MORE
SUPER SOCKS

Further sock techniques with "Winwick Mum"

Christine Perry

More Super Socks

First edition published in the United Kingdom
September 2018 by Christine Perry

Publisher: Winwick Mum

ISBN-13: 978-1-9998919-1-6

As always, my biggest hugs , love and thanks go to my family.
I am blessed with a husband and daughters who make molehills out of my mountains,
love me unconditionally despite my filling the house with yarn and
know that there is no better sock in the world than a hand-knitted sock.
Or at least, that's what they tell me ☺

My wonderful friends Sally Tomkins, Sonia Christie and Lucy of Attic24
for friendship, humour, wisdom, chocolate-sharing and sometimes just a straight talking-to.
I would be lost without all of you.

The members of the Winwick Mum Sockalong and Knit n Natter Facebook groups
who remind me on a daily basis that knitting has no language barriers and that there's
always something new to learn.

Helen Birch (helenelizabethbyarntec@gmail.com) and Lynne Rowe (LPP10@sky.com)
for tech editing my patterns and helping me to become a better pattern writer,
and Nicola Grossman for another fabulous book cover (www.nicolagrossman.co.uk).

Thank you! xx

CONTENTS

INTRODUCTION

My name is Christine and I write a blog called *Winwick Mum* (you can find it at www.winwickmum.co.uk). It all began with a monthly contribution (my Monthly Musing) for the Winwick St Oswald's Church newsletter and has gradually grown to become a blog about all sorts of things that interest me about my daily life and life as a Mum.

I'm also rather obsessed with sock knitting and, in particular, helping other people to discover that it's not as difficult as they might think. The blog has become a place for me to share my free hand-knitted sock patterns and in 2015, I published a series of basic sock-knitting tutorials on my blog, determined to show people that knitting a pair of socks is within everyone's reach. I called them the "Winwick Mum Sockalong" and I thought it would be great if just a few people found them and discovered that they could knit socks after all.

Three years later, thousands of people have knitted thousands of pairs of socks using my Sockalong tutorials. It looks like my initial joke of "taking over the world one sock at a time" might not be such a daft idea, and the tutorials are still available for free on my blog if you want to take a look.

The Sockalong was always intended to be used as a springboard; a starting point to discovering the incredible range of sock patterns that are available, particularly on websites such as Ravelry (www.ravelry.com) as once you understand how a basic sock is constructed, it's much easier to read other patterns – a foot is a foot and most socks are generally constructed in the same way. However, I soon realised that there is still a huge gap between a basic sock and a patterned sock and sometimes knowing how a sock is constructed simply isn't enough. Rather than a springboard, this book is designed to be a bridge, another step forwards in knowledge which will bring those other sock patterns a little bit closer and make them seem less daunting.

I have taken four knitting techniques which are often the theme of sock patterns (perhaps with the exception of intarsia but it's fun to knit and useful to know how to do) and broken them down into easy steps to encourage everybody to let go of the safety handrail of the basic Sockalong sock and give them a try. After all, if we're taking over the world with our hand-knitted socks, we might as well be able to wear ones with any pattern we like knitted into them, right?! ☺

SUPER SOCKS

Super Socks is the paperback and e-book version of the online Sockalong tutorials. Not everyone wants to or can be online all the time, and sometimes it's just nice to have a large, physical book to prop open or make notes in. You'll see it mentioned from time to time in this book, and if you've never knitted socks before – whilst there's no reason that you can't launch straight into one of these pairs as your first – you'll find it a handy reference if you get stuck.

The difference between the book version of the tutorials and the online version is that the book version is divided into sections by needle type whereas the online version is divided by sock section. This is because the tutorials were originally published over three weeks, but if you're using the book then it's easier to have all of the information for the needle that you're using in one place.

Super Socks won 3rd place in the Favourite Knitting Book category 2016 British Knitting Awards and at the time of writing, over 5,000 copies have been sold since it was first published three years ago. You'll find it on Amazon and in some local yarn shops and I sell it directly through my blog, but do ask your local book seller if they can order a copy for you too – I firmly believe we should support our local shops whenever we can!

ABOUT THE PATTERNS

This book is designed for people who know how to knit a basic sock but are yet to dip their toes into the water of adding patterns to their socks. Written and charted patterns can look daunting if you've never used them before but once you understand how they're written, you see that they're not that inaccessible at all. You might have thought that about knitting a basic sock once, but here you are … ☺

The patterns are all based on my basic 4ply "Sockalong" sock pattern, which is knitted from the top down and grafted at the toes using Kitchener stitch. I also use a heel flap and gusset-type heel which I believe is the easiest for people to get to grips with – heels can seem particularly baffling to someone who hasn't knitted socks before and my aim is always to write patterns which are possible to finish rather than the socks being thrown across the room in disgust. Once you've got the hang of one type of heel, it's easy to try out different types (and there are more than a few) to see which one you like best. Most of the parts of a sock are interchangeable which makes them really versatile projects that can be adapted to suit any feet and any knitting preference.

In this book, I've included four tutorials which each look at a different pattern technique. They are cables, lace, intarsia and colourwork; each of these (with possibly the exception of intarsia which isn't very common) are regularly incorporated into sock patterns and once you have grasped the basics of how each one works – including how to read the patterns and charts that go with them – then you will be able to go and try out more patterns. The tutorials include plenty of pictures and also video links to various sections of the sock so that you can see exactly how to work each section of the sock. You'll notice that two of the patterns in this section do not have separate sizes for you to work to: this is quite deliberate as the sock is easily adjusted to different sizes using the Sock Stitch Calculation that you'll find on page 9. I think it's always good to know how to make your own adjustments and I'm giving you the opportunity here to practice!

In the second section of the book are four brand new and exclusive patterns that won't be available anywhere else. Each one uses the techniques that you'll have practiced with the tutorials and although there are still photos to go with each pattern, there isn't as much tutorial detail – the idea is that you can check back with the tutorials if you need to but you have the opportunity to use a pattern that is more like one that you'll find online or in a pattern book.

By the time you've worked your way through these patterns, you'll be raring to find out what else is out there! ☺

ABOUT THE YARNS

The yarns used for the socks in this book are all British yarns from sheep which graze on British fields and their fleece spun here in Britain, often no more than a few miles from where the sheep are kept.

Some time ago, I became really interested in the different breeds of sheep that are farmed in Britain and whether the yarns that were produced from their fleece would be suitable for socks even if they weren't specifically made to be sock yarns. Traditionally, sock yarns contain nylon to make them more hardwearing, and in addition, some yarns are treated with the patented "Superwash" process which removes the scales from the fleece (wool fibre is very much like our human hair with scales along its length and it's these scales that cause felting when they're washed in water that's too hot) either by blasting them with chlorine gas or coating them in plastic, resulting in a yarn that is smooth to knit with, which takes up dye beautifully so is often used by hand-dyers and – most importantly for some people – produces a yarn which will survive the washing machine and tumble dryer. There is also anecdotal evidence that some people with lanolin or wool allergies have found that superwash yarns don't affect them in the same way as other yarns which allows them to wear wool, so the process has certainly made a huge beneficial difference to the yarn industry and also the wider clothing industry.

However, superwash is not a process appreciated by all knitters because of the chemicals involved, and not all yarns require nylon to give them strength. It is possible to have machine washable yarns that are not superwash treated and it is also possible to knit "no nylon" socks which rely on the characteristics of the fleece and the blend of fibres within the yarn to provide strength. With the growing interest in reducing plastic consumption, I was intrigued to find out more about the options that are available to knitters.

I discovered that the strength of a yarn is based on the "staple length" of the fibre that's used to make it. Staple length is simply the length of the fleece from where it's cut from the sheep to the very end, and the longer the better.

This is Poll Dorset fleece and you can see that the length is over 2 inches (5 cm) which is perfect for spinning into a worsted yarn where the lengths of fibre are spun smoothly together; shorter pieces of wool mean that the fibres won't lie smoothly in the same direction and will stick out, resulting in a woollier yarn which is not as comfortable to wear. There are lots of breeds of sheep which have fleece with a long staple length and these fibres can also be blended with other fibres such as silk or mohair (also known as "Nature's Nylon") to make the yarn stronger without the addition of nylon.

There are a few words of caution if you're planning to try out your own no-nylon yarn discoveries: firstly, the softer the yarn, the more quickly it will wear out so 100% Merino or Alpaca definitely needs something else with it to give it more strength. However, it is possible to have beautifully soft yarns which don't contain nylon but are suitable for socks so don't give up hope! Look for yarns which are spun from named breeds rather than just "wool": longwool breeds such as Blue-faced Leicester, Wensleydale and Teeswater are popular choices, but there are sheep with closely curled fleeces such as the Poll Dorset which also produce fleece suitable for socks. Secondly, these socks do require a bit more care than those knitted from commercial yarns: experiments have shown me that whilst hand-washing is the optimum way to care for your socks, the yarns that I have tried out can be washed in the washing machine but I wouldn't recommend a programme other than a gentle hand wash.

I've been reviewing the yarns that I've used so far on my blog at www.winwickmum.co.uk/p/no-nylon-sock-yarn-reviews.html. My findings so far have been very positive and I would encourage everybody to look further than the "sock yarn" section of their yarn shops to see what other yarns will feel fabulous on your feet. My belief is that the more we know about the sheep, their fleece, the manufacturing processes and the companies that provide the yarn, whether they are large manufacturers or small independent companies, the more connected to our knitting and to the wool industry as a whole we become. Very often, there is little profit in fleece for sheep farmers but there is a growing movement to reverse this trend, to bring British sheep breeds to the forefront of knitters' attention and to support our home-grown wool industry.

As knitters, we are no longer just end buyers of yarn in a shop but we are a vital part of the industry, our buying decisions are informed by more than just price or colour and we are helping everybody – farmers, spinners, dyers, designers and yarn shop owners – along the way. It feels good to be part of it.

* * *

The socks in the first tutorial section of the book are all British no-nylon yarns, and the patterns in the second section of the book are all still British yarns but they are not all no-nylon ones. There's no obligation to use these same yarns as all of these patterns can be used with any 4ply yarn (or even a different weight if you choose to adapt the pattern for that).

Easy Cable Socks – Northern Yarn Poll Dorset Lambswool 4ply: This yarn was produced by Kate Makin of Northern Yarn who wanted to work with the farmers that she had got to know around her local area of Lancaster. Poll Dorsets are sturdy sheep that live on the Lancashire hills and are outside in all weathers. Their coats look short and closely curled but as you can see from the previous photo, the length of their fleece makes it perfect for spinning into yarn. The yarn was spun at the Halifax Spinning Mill using traditional machinery. (**www.northernyarn.co.uk**)

Easy Lace Socks – Doulton Flock Border Leicester 4ply: Border Leicester sheep are very distinctive with huge ears that stand up like rabbits' ears. They're very pretty! They also have a fleece that looks short and closely curled but which provides a long staple length. The Doulton Flock is the largest herd of pedigree Border Leicester sheep in the UK and every sheep is allowed to grow old as the flock's owner, Ellie Stokeld, refuses to sell them for meat. The yarn is spun at Laxton's mill in North Yorkshire, not far from where the flock is based. (**www.doultonborderleicesteryarn.com**)

Patchwork Socks – The Little Grey Sheep Stein Fine 4ply: Stein Fine sheep are sheep bred specifically for their fleece by Emma Boyles and her shepherd, Susie Parish, at The Little Grey Sheep farm in Hampshire. The original Swedish Gotland sheep on the farm were crossed with first Shetland and then Merino sheep to produce this soft, lustrous yarn which is hand-dyed on the farm. The company was named after the original sheep on the farm – the little grey Gotland sheep - and there is still a line of those sheep kept for their fleeces which are also spun and sold. The Stein Fine yarn is spun in Devon. (**www.thelittlegreysheep.co.uk**)

Easy Colourwork Socks – Freehold Yarn Co Autumn 4ply: Another yarn from Lancaster, this yarn is a blend of 75% Blue-faced Leicester and 25% Gotland. The Gotland sheep have fleece with bouncy ringlets and the Blue-faced Leicester has longer, dreadlock-type fleece (think Dougal from *The Magic Roundabout!*). Amy, the owner of the shop, decided to create the yarn after watching a TV programme about coloured sheep fleece being less desirable than white fleece which are easier to dye, and set about making her own yarn with a coloured base. The wool is purchased and scoured in Bradford and spun at Laxton's mill in Yorkshire. (**www.freeholdyarnco.com**)

Drunken Cable Socks – Baa Ram Ewe Titus 4ply: This yarn is a blend of 50% Wensleydale (similar to the Blue-faced Leicester to look at with it's long dreadlocks), 20% Blue-faced Leicester and 30% British Alpaca which gives a yarn that is strong enough for socks thanks to the long staple length of the longwool sheep, but soft as well thanks to the Alpaca content. It's spun specially for Baa Ram Ewe in Yorkshire at a mill very close to where Baa Ram Ewe is based and the yarn is named after Sir Titus Salt, the British philanthropist and mill owner who created the "model village" of Saltaire in Yorkshire as a place for his workers to live. (**www.baaramwewe.co.uk**)

Beatrice Socks – Eden Cottage Yarns Milburn 4ply: Eden Cottage Yarns is owned by Victoria Magnus and is based in Wetherby, Yorkshire, where Victoria has her hand-dyeing studio. Milburn 4ply is a blend of 85% British Blued-faced Leicester and 15% silk, which is what gives the yarn it's strength. One of the only yarns not to be dyed on the premises, it is dyed locally in small batches to Victoria's exact specifications. Milburn is a superwash wool which means that it is machine washable. (**www.edencottageyarns.co.uk**)

Flow Through Socks – West Yorkshire Spinners Signature 4ply: A family firm based in Keighley, North Yorkshire, West Yorkshire Spinners pride themselves on spinning and selling British yarns and are able to trace the provenance of the fleece they use back to the farms. Signature 4ply is a blend of 75% British wool including 35% Blue-faced Leicester which gives the yarn a lovely "bloom" and 25% nylon to make them more hard-wearing. The yarn is not superwash treated but is machine-washable.

Rainbow Zig Zag Socks – West Yorkshire Spinners Signature 4ply: Another pair of socks using West Yorkshire Spinners yarn. They have a large range of colours which makes their yarn a great choice for socks, including the extremely popular "Rum Paradise" colourway which gives these socks their rainbow stripes.

West Yorkshire Spinners yarn is available through local yarn shops (always support your local yarn shop if you can!) or **www.wyspinners.com** for overseas orders.

GAUGE AND SOCK SIZING

"Tension swatches? I never bother with those!"

If that sounds like you, we need to have a chat! Tension swatches are not the most exciting things in the world, but they do actually have a use and believe it or not, just ten minutes spent swatching and checking your gauge can make all the difference between a sock that fits and a sock that doesn't.

I've lost count of the number of people who say to me, "I haven't got time to do that, just tell me how many to cast on for a size 5 foot". This is where it all goes a bit wrong for some sock knitters and they wonder why their socks don't fit. It's simple: my size 5 feet might be the same *length* as your size 5 feet, but our feet might not actually be the same *size*. We might have feet that are narrower or wider; we might have to compensate for swollen ankles or muscly calves. Getting the perfect-fitting sock is possible, but only if you measure your feet and measure your knitting.

If you've never done this before, you'll be pleased to know that it's easy. Ten minutes, twenty at the most, that's all, and then you've got your measurements for any future pairs of socks too. (Although obviously if anything changes with your feet, then you'll need to re-measure!)

Working a tension swatch

This is the method that I use for socks as it's the stitches per inch that are most important here. For any other garment, swatch to get the size recommended in the pattern or on the ball band.

Start by casting on a number of stitches using the yarn that you want to knit your socks with and the needles that you're going to knit with. I tend to cast on about 20-30 stitches so that I've got a decent-sized swatch to work with. It's best to do this on double pointed needles as we're going to replicate knitting in the round on two needles using knitting expert Elizabeth Zimmerman's swatching technique.

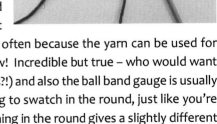

In this photo, I've cast on with 4ply on 2.5 mm needles. This is the standard needle size for socks, but we'll talk more about that in a minute. You might wonder why the ball band for your yarn gives a different size but that's often because the yarn can be used for

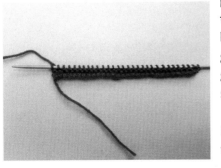

projects other than socks (I know! Incredible but true – who would want to knit anything other than socks?!) and also the ball band gauge is usually knitted flat whereas you're going to swatch in the round, just like you're going to knit your socks. Swatching in the round gives a slightly different gauge; it's not a huge difference but could be enough to make your socks slightly less well fitting.

Next, knit three rows to give yourself an edge that's less likely to roll up when you come to measure your knitting.

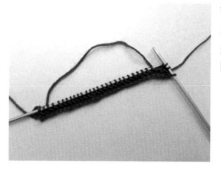

When you get to the end of the third row, instead of turning your knitting and working back along the stitches as you would do for a normal garter or stocking stitch swatch, you're going to bring the yarn back round to the beginning of your stitches leaving a long loop and knit the row again.

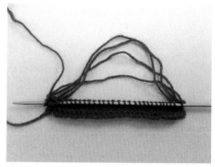

Every time you get to the end of your row, bring the yarn back to the beginning so that you're always knitting on the right side of your work.

By doing this, you're only ever working knit stitches which is exactly what you do when you knit in the round, and this will give you your "in the round" tension. It looks messy on the back but it does the job!

Continue to bring the yarn around the back of your knitting and work enough rows until you have a piece of knitting that you are able to measure easily.

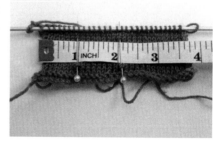

The standard gauge for 4ply on 2.5 mm needles in the round is 30 sts to 4 inches (10 cm) which works out at 7.5 stitches per inch. It's not always easy to get that exact number but as long as you're getting about 7-8 stitches per inch, your socks should turn out fine.

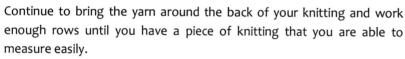

Count your stitches within 1 inch

If you're getting too many stitches, try a bigger needle and if you're not getting enough, try a smaller needle until you get the right size.

Once you have worked out the number of stitches per inch, you're half way there. Now you need to measure around the ball of your foot (that's the widest part of your foot just under your toes) and if you know that you have wider ankles or calves, take a measurement there too.

Now we're going to apply those numbers to the Sock Stitch Calculation. Got a pen and paper? OK, let's go!

SOCK STITCH CALCULATION

Working out the number of stitches you need for your sock

This method can be adapted to any sock yarn and any size of feet. The number of stitches that you choose to cast on must always be divisible by 4, so choose the nearest multiple of 4 to the result that you get from your stitch calculation.

1   Measure around the ball of your foot (in inches) and multiply that measurement by the number of stitches per inch from your swatch. In my case, it would be 8 (foot measurement) x 8 (stitches per inch) = 64

2   Next, you need to allow for the negative ease (stretch in the knitted fabric) so take 10% off the total – in my case, 10% of 64 stitches would be 6.4 but it's easiest to round it up or down to the nearest whole number. This would make the new calculation 64 (original number of stitches) – 6 (10% negative ease) = 58.

3   Remember that the number of stitches that you cast on needs to be a multiple of 4, so for my sock I could cast on either 56 or 60 stitches – I think that 56 would be just bit too tight so I am going to choose to cast on 60 stitches. It's generally better for your sock fabric to be tighter than, say, for a jumper as that makes it more hard-wearing, but you don't want it so tight that it pulls across your foot.

And that's it! If you have taken extra measurements for your ankle or calf, work those out in exactly the same way and compare them to your foot measurement. If they're bigger or smaller, you can adapt your sock by casting on more or less stitches and increasing or decreasing as you need to. I find that it's easiest to do this at the gusset by decreasing to more or less than the original cast on number but you can take a view depending on the feet you're knitting for.

In the end, the gauge becomes a matter of preference – some people like tighter socks, others prefer looser socks and as you complete more pairs, you will see which you prefer for yourself. The nice thing about hand-knits is that you can try your socks on at every stage to make sure they are going to fit perfectly.

You can use this calculation for any weight of yarn and the pattern and tutorials will also work with any type of yarn, so there is no limit to the socks you can make! Some of the sock patterns will be easier to adapt to multiple sizes within the sock than others, but again you can take a view on this by looking at the pattern before you start.

ADDITIONAL HELPFUL HINTS

- If you've got a high instep, work a longer heel flap and longer gusset decreases to make your sock fit better. Don't forget that you can try your sock on at any time, although if you're using a short circular needle or DPNs you may want to put your stitches on a spare piece of yarn or a stitch holder so that you don't lose any stitches whilst you do so.

- Many knitters find that they get a hole at the point where their picked up gusset stitches meet the top of the foot stitches. Avoid this by picking up one extra stitch down the heel flap but make sure that you pick up the leg of a proper stitch, not the bar in between two stitches. You can also knit into the back of that stitch to twist it if it feels as if it will still be a bit loose.

- Keep SSK decreases on the gusset straighter by knitting into the back of the stitch on the alternate knit rounds. You don't have to continue doing this once you have finished the gusset decreases.

- I always recommend that you cast on with a size larger needles – you'll see them marked "optional" in the patterns – so that the cuff isn't too tight. I use a cable cast on which isn't the stretchiest cast on to use so working with bigger needles helps; you can use any cast on that you like so if you've got a stretchier one that you like, you don't need to use the bigger needles unless you want to.

- You can knit some of the patterns in this book using leftover yarn rather than buying whole new balls. To make sure that you've got enough, weigh the leftovers before you start to make sure that you've got at least 100g, which is usually more than enough for the average pair of socks. You can even weigh a sock that you've already knitted for a more exact figure, but do be sure to allow extra yarn just in case!

- I've given the number of rounds or rows that I knitted on a sock just as a guide. They will change depending on your own tension and the yarn that you're using so don't worry that you have to follow them; it's always better to work to a given size than a row or round count. I just put them there so that if you're on round 20 of your foot and you know that I knitted at least 40 rounds, you can see how much further you need to go before you measure for your own foot.

- 100g of yarn should be enough for even a large pair of socks but if in doubt, always buy an extra ball – you'll always be able to use it up! If buying a skein, it's best to check the length of the skein as well as the weight as it will vary from skein to skein – anything that's around 400m long should be plenty, but do take a view based on the size of feet you are knitting for.

TUTORIALS

Easy Cable Socks – page 12

Easy Lace Socks – page 24

Patchwork Socks – page 37

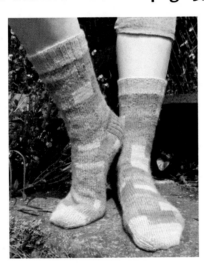

Easy Colourwork Socks – page 51

These tutorials were originally published on the *Winwick Mum* blog and are designed to be a next step up from the basic Sockalong sock, and a bridge between that and other published patterns.

The assumption is that you know how to knit a basic sock before you tackle these patterns, but don't worry if you haven't – you should still be able to follow along with the pattern but if you want to check out my basic 4ply sock pattern, you can find it and the Sockalong tutorials on my *Winwick Mum* blog (www.winwickmum.co.uk) or in the *Super Socks* book.

EASY CABLE SOCKS

What is it about a cable that looks so special in a sock? I don't know, but I think cables might be my very favourite type of design feature in knitting. I just love the smooth lines of them, they look just like ropes - you can see why cables work so well in fishermen's jumpers!

These socks are designed with two cables down the front to give you chance to get used to knitting cables and also to reading a chart if you've never done that before. It's really not as scary as you might think and it will open up a whole new range of patterns that you can try out.

This tutorial has both photos and videos to go along with the written instructions to help you. I've put the video links after the photos so you'll need to get to the end of each section to find them - and I'd recommend that you read each section first anyway before you start knitting so that you're sure you're happy with what you're doing.

The cables in this sock are very simple in construction, they're only four stitches which twist around each other.

This tutorial shows you how to create the cable with a cable needle. There is a method for cabling without a needle but I'm not going to cover that here - you can always look online if you want to find out more.

Seriously, I can't get enough of these cables! I think it's a kind of magic to see the yarn twist around itself like this!

You don't need a cable needle for this crossed rib heel - you can complete that with your usual needles. Doesn't this stitch go well with the main rib section? I love the way that you can combine different stitches and techniques to create something that looks as if it should always have been that way!

Before we launch into the pattern itself, I want to talk to you about the chart that's included in the pattern along with the written instructions. Some people like charts and others run from them as if their pants are on fire. They are really not that bad, trust me! Think of a chart as a road map, directing your knitting as a map would direct your car on a journey.

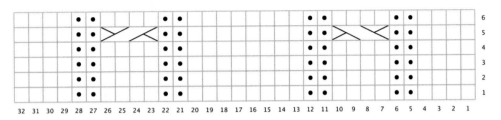

This is the chart for the Easy Cable Socks. It doesn't look that scary, does it? Let's see what it's telling us.

Firstly, you can see that there are 6 rows (these are the numbers going up the right-hand side) and 32 stitches (these are the numbers along the bottom). The numbers go outwards from that very first square on the bottom right hand side because that's where you'll start from, but we'll talk about that in a minute.

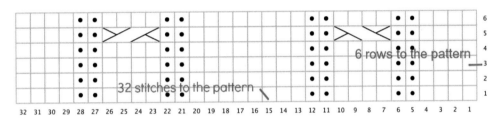

Here's the key for the Easy Cable Socks chart. Every chart is created by a combination of symbols, and there is always a key to tell you what those symbols mean. Remember the road map? You wouldn't be able to read it without a key to help you and this is the same.

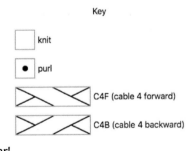

There will usually be written instructions within the pattern that tell you how to do any special stitches (charts are not just for cables, you'll see them in lace, intarsia and colourwork patterns too), so don't worry if you don't know how to do the stitch that's been charted - the designer should make everything clear!

And remember that I said you always start reading the chart from the bottom right hand corner?

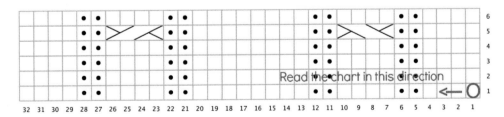

Using the key to tell you which stitches to knit, you will complete the first row of the chart like this:

For row 2, you'll go back to the right-hand side and read along the row 2 line, and the same for row 3 and so on. Some people like to mark off the rows as they go along so that they can see where they're up to - you can use a ruler or write on the pattern. If you're using a pattern with a chart (paid for or free) and don't want to write on your original pattern, it's OK to make a copy of the chart for your own personal use as long as you don't share it with anyone else for copyright reasons.

As well as telling you which stitches to use in the pattern, the chart also tells you where to place your stitches. Looking at our pattern, you can see that the cable stitches are only on row 5, and the symbol shows you which direction your cable stitch will go in (cable stitches usually go forwards or backwards).

Can you see that the symbols show the cables leaning towards each other?

Now let's have a look at how it all knits up ...

Can you see how the chart and the knitted cables are showing the same thing? It's really not as hard as you think!

If you want to adjust the size of your sock, you may want to adjust the size of your pattern panel too. That's really easy to do. If you look at the chart, you can see that there's a panel of 8 knitted stitches in the middle and two panels of 4 knitted stitches on either side. You can easily add and remove stitches from those panels to fit the number of stitches for your sock.

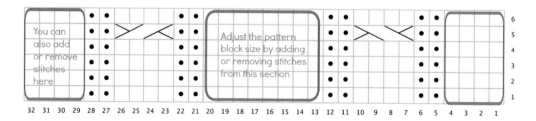

If you change the stitches in the side panels, remember that you'll have to do the same for both sides or your pattern block will be off-centre!

OK then, that should be everything you need to get started with the pattern. Are you ready? Then we'll begin!

Easy Cable Socks

These cabled socks are constructed as top-down socks with a gusset heel. The heel is knitted in crossed rib stitch, which creates a durable, cushioned heel. This pattern will create a medium-sized sock but can be adjusted for other sizes.

Gauge   30 stitches to 4 inches (10 cm) in stocking stitch (worked in the round) on 2.5 mm needles

Materials

2.5 mm needles - short circular needle, DPNs (Double Pointed Needles) or an 80 cm circular for magic loop
1 x 100g skein of Northern Yarn 100% Poll Dorset Lambswool
1 set DPNs size 3.0 mm (optional)
1 set DPNs size 2.5 mm (not required for magic loop)
1 cable needle
Stitch markers
Wool needle

Abbreviations

C4B	Slip the next two stitches on the left hand needle onto a cable needle and hold at the back of your work. Knit the next two stitches on the left hand needle then knit the stitches from the cable needle.
C4F	Slip the next two stitches on the left hand needle onto a cable needle and hold at the front of your work. Knit the next two stitches on the left hand needle then knit the two stitches from the cable needle.
K	Knit
P	Purl
K2tog	Knit two stitches together
Slip 1	Slip 1 stitch purlwise
SSK	Slip the first stitch on the left hand needle knitwise onto the right hand needle, slip the second stitch on the left hand needle purlwise onto the right hand needle, slip both stitches back onto the left hand needle and knit together through back loop
St(s)	Stitch(es)
( )	Repeat instructions inside brackets

Pattern notes

- It is often easier to cast on using DPNs before changing to the short circular needle and joining into the round and so this pattern has been written for this method. If you want to use magic loop you will be able to cast on with the larger circular needle if you prefer to do so, but remember not to pull your cast on stitches too tight. If you use DPNs, you might find it easiest to cast on and work 2 rows before dividing the stitches across the needles.

- Use lifelines in your work as often as you feel you need to – there's no limit to the number of them that you can use in one sock! You can find instructions for creating lifelines on page 33.
- Mark each row on your chart as you work it – it's easier to work out where you're up to if you have to put your knitting down for a while.
- If you have to take your work back, unravel one round at a time and don't forget to amend your chart so that you know where you're up to.

Adjusting the size: The cable pattern is 8 stitches wide and will work with any weight of yarn and any number of stitches that you cast on, although if you may need to alter the size of the cable pattern. To adjust the size for this sock, simply add 4 stitches to your usual cast-on number of stitches to accommodate the cable pulling the knitted fabric inwards and alter the number that you cast on by adding or removing stitches in blocks of 4 from the cast on total - you can find the sock stitch calculation on page 9. If you normally cast on 60 stitches, you will cast on 64; if you normally cast on 64, you will cast on 68 and so on. Then work out how many stitches you need to add or remove to position the pattern block in the centre of your "top of the foot" stitches (the pattern block will always be half the number that you cast on). See page 14 for the diagram on where to add or remove stitches.

<u>Pattern</u> – make both the same

Cast on 64 stitches using 3.0 mm needles.

Row 1:   (K2, P2), repeat to end, turn.
Row 2:   (K2, P2), repeat to end, turn.

Change to 2.5 mm needles. At this point, change to a short circular needle, magic loop or divide the stitches across DPNs and join into a circle, place marker. It's easy to change to the circular needle simply by knitting off the DPNs onto the new needle.

Continue in K2, P2 rib for 14 more rounds or until desired length of rib.

 Here's the video link for the cable cast on, transferring to a short circular need and joining into the round: http://bit.ly/EasyCableCastOn

<u>Cable pattern</u>

Start the cable pattern on the next round. I'm going to give you the pattern instructions first and then show you how the cable is worked below. The cable block is worked in sections of 6 rounds and instructions on how to work the cable are as follows:

Rounds 1-4:   K4, P2, K4, P2, K8, P2, K4, P2, K4, knit to marker.
Round 5:   K4, P2, C4F, P2, K8, P2, C4B, P2, K4, knit to marker.
Round 6:   K4, P2, K4, P2, K8, P2, K4, P2, K4, knit to marker.

If you want to use the chart, the pattern is as follows:

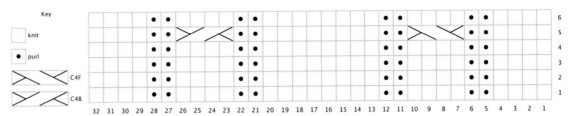

As you can see from the key, the reason the stitch is called C4F is because it's a cable stitch (C), there are four stitches in the block (4) and you're bringing the stitches forward (F). This is the point where you'll need your cable needle.

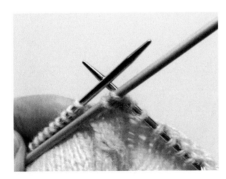

1 To complete your **C4F** stitch, slip the first two stitches of the block purl-wise onto your cable needle and hold those stitches in front of your work.

2 Now, keeping the cable needle in front of your work, knit the next two stitches of the cable block.

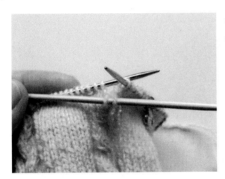

3 Next, you need to knit the two stitches off the cable needle and back onto your right-hand needle. Don't worry if it feels a bit tight, it will sort itself out on the next round.

You've completed your cable stitch! You can see how the stitches have twisted to form the cable. Easy, eh?

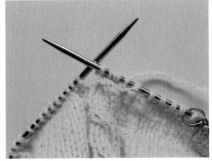

Now I'm going to show you how to do the C4B stitch. It's very similar to the C4F - it's a cable stitch (C), there are four stitches in the block (4) but this time you're taking the stitches backwards (B). You'll need your cable needle for this stitch too.

1 To complete your **C4B** stitch, slip the first two stitches of the block purl-wise onto your cable needle and hold those stitches at the back of your work.

2 Now, keeping the cable needle at the back of your work, knit the next two stitches of the cable block.

3 Next, you need to knit the two stitches off the cable needle and back onto your right-hand needle. Don't worry if it feels a bit tight, it will sort itself out on the next round.

You've completed your next cable stitch! You can see how the stitches have twisted to form the cable but this time they're twisting in the opposite direction.

 Here's the video link for the C4F and C4B cables:
http://bit.ly/CreatingCables

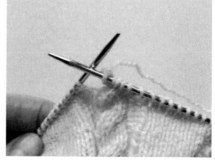

Continue to knit each round until you reach your desired length before the start of your heel (for me, this was 9 blocks of the 6 round pattern which makes 70 rounds including the rib) ending with round 6. You can finish on a different row of the pattern if you want to, but you'll need to remember what it is for the next section.

Heel Flap

The heel flap for this sock is created with crossed rib stitches, which are knitted without a cable needle. There are 3 stitches in this pattern. If you have more or less than 64 stitches in your heel flap, you will need to either add or remove crossed stitches. If you prefer to make a heel stitch heel flap rather than a crossed rib stitch one, you can follow the instructions in the Easy Lace Socks pattern on page 24 to do this.

To start the heel flap, we need to knit across the top of the foot stitches to work on the back section of stitches:

Next round: K4, P2, K4, P2, K8, P2, K4, P2, K4 (these are the top of the foot stitches from row 1 of the cable pattern – if you finished on a different row or altered the pattern block, use the correct line from the chart to keep your pattern in sequence) and create the heel flap as follows:

Change to 2.5 mm DPNs if you are using a short circular needle. You are going to create the heel flap from half the number of stitches that you cast on, so if you have cast on more or less than 64 stitches, remember to adjust the number of stitches when you start the heel flap.

This is how you work the crossed rib stitch (**cross2RK**):

Row 1:   K2, (cross2RK, P1), until you have 32 stitches on your needle, turn.
Row 2:   Slip 1, P to end, turn.
Row 3:   Slip 1, K1, (cross2RK, P1), to end, turn.

1 To make your crossed rib stitch, start by knitting into the **second** stitch on your left-hand needle like this …

2 Pull the yarn through but don't try to slide the stitches off the needle …

3 Instead, knit into the **first** stitch on the left-hand needle. It's a bit fiddly until you get used to it so relax your hands and pull a bit more yarn through from the first stitch if you need to ...

4 Pull the yarn through ...

5 And slide both stitches off your left-hand needle onto the right-hand needle.

Repeat rows 2 and 3 until your heel flap measures approximately 2 ½ inches (6 cm), finishing on row 3 (for me, this was 29 rows but it will depend on your yarn). If you want to make the heel flap longer, continue knitting rows 2 and 3 until you reach the desired length, but remember that you will need to pick up more stitches to create the gusset.

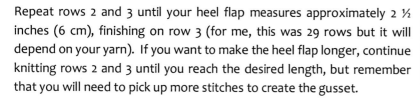

This what your heel flap will look like on the outside ...

and on the inside. Don't worry if your heel flap seems to lean to one side, it will straighten up as you pick up the gusset stitches.

 This is the video link for creating the heel flap:
http://bit.ly/EasyCableHeelFlap

Turn heel

Now we're up to the fun part! This is where your sock starts to look like a sock. Some people do worry about this bit, but just take it slowly and you'll be fine.

Note: For a larger or smaller sock, you will need to alter the number of purl stitches in the first row of the heel (marked in bold below), increasing by 1 stitch for each block of 4 stitches extra that you cast on, or decreasing by 1 stitch for each block of 4 stitches less than 64 stitches. For example, if you cast on 68 stitches, your first row would be Slip 1, **P18**, P2tog, P1, turn.

Row 1:   Slip 1, **P17,** P2tog, P1, turn.
Row 2:   Slip 1, K5, SSK, K1, turn.
Row 3:   Slip 1, P6, P2tog, P1, turn.
Row 4:   Slip 1, K7, SSK, K1, turn.

Continue in this way, adding one stitch between slip stitch and SSK or P2tog on each row (ie, Row 5: Slip 1, **P8**, P2tog, P1; Row 6: Slip 1, **K9**, SSK, K1, etc) until all of the heel stitches are used.

 The video tutorial for the heel turn is here: http://bit.ly/EasyCableHeelTurn

Knit across the heel stitches if required to bring you to the left-hand side of the heel ready to pick up and knit 1 stitch for every 2 rows knitted. Remember that if you made the heel flap bigger you will need to pick up more stitches. Knit across the top of the foot **in pattern - you will be on round 2** (or the next row after whichever one you knitted across the top of the foot stitches - I usually knit across these stitches on my circular needle at this point), place marker, then pick up and knit 1 stitch for every 2 rows knitted up the other side of the heel. Knit across the top of the heel then shape gusset as below, placing your second marker at the end of the first set of picked up stitches.

Note: If you are using DPNs and/or have placed your top of the foot stitches on a stitch holder, you can arrange the needles as follows: Needle 1 for stitches across heel, Needle 2 for picked-up stitches down left side of foot, Needle 3 for stitches across top of the foot (knit stitches off the stitch holder if required), Needle 4 for picked up stitches on the right side of the foot. You may find that stitch markers are not required at first.

Shape gusset

Round 1:   K to 3 sts before the marker, K2tog, K1, slip marker, knit in pattern to next marker, slip marker, K1, SSK, K to marker.
Round 2:   Slip marker, knit in pattern to next marker, slip marker, knit to 3 sts before marker.
Round 3:   K2tog, K1, slip marker, knit in pattern to next marker, slip marker, K1, SSK, K to marker.

Repeat rounds 2 and 3 to shape the gusset and continue in this way, decreasing by two stitches at the gusset on every other row until there are 64 stitches on the needle.

You can see the line of the gusset quite clearly here:

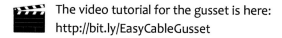
The video tutorial for the gusset is here:
http://bit.ly/EasyCableGusset

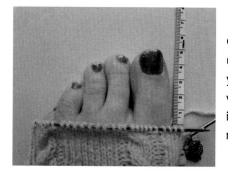

Once you have 64 stitches again, continue to knit each round in pattern until you reach approximately 2 inches (5 cm) before the desired length of your sock ready to start the toes. (For me, this was 11 blocks of the pattern which is 66 rounds.) You'll need to use two markers for the toes to indicate the decreases, so you'll want to be sure that you get them in the right place.

This should be quite easy as you've had the pattern block across the top of your foot so you should be able to see where they should go, but do take a minute to check. Don't be afraid to try your sock on before decreasing for the toes and when you measure your sock, make sure that you are standing up as you need your full weight on your foot. Sometimes you have to do more rounds than you might think to get the length, but it's worth make sure that your sock is the right length for your foot otherwise it will pull against your toes and also pull your heel under your foot – neither of which are very comfortable!

Toes

At some point whilst decreasing for the toes, if you are using a short circular needle you may need to change back to DPNs as the number of stitches becomes too small for the circular or alternatively, you could use a larger circular needle for magic loop. It's up to you when you choose to do that, and how you distribute the stitches across the needles; just keep following the pattern as set below.

You can choose whether to continue the cables to the ends of the toes or to knit this section in plain knit. Create the toes as follows:

Round 1:   K1, SSK, K26 sts (in pattern if desired), K2tog, K1, place marker, K1, SSK, K26 sts, K2tog, K1
Round 2:   Knit one round, slipping markers as you come to them
Round 3:   K1, SSK, K to 3 sts before marker (in pattern if desired), K2tog, K1, slip marker, K1, SSK, K to 3 sts before marker, K2tog, K1

Repeat rounds 2 and 3 until you have 28 stitches left and divide these between two needles so that front and back of your socks match (14 stitches on each needle).

Grafting the toes with Kitchener stitch

This is another part of the sock-creation that some people aren't so keen on, but again it's not too bad if you take it slowly. There is a separate section on grafting the toes with Kitchener stitch on page 112 .

 The video on grafting the toes is here: http://bit.ly/EasyCableKitchener

Finally, sew the seam together at the cuff of the sock where you knitted your first two rib rows on DPNs, tightening it up if you need to and your first sock is done!

Now all you need to do is make a second sock and your pair of Easy Cable Socks is finished!

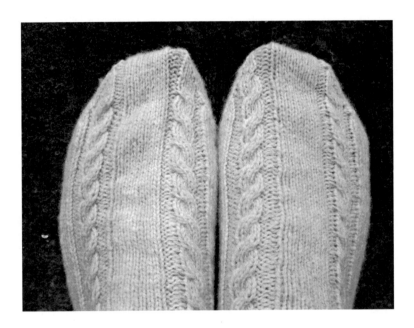

EASY LACE SOCKS

Lace knitting is the perfect way to show off your knitting skills. It always looks as if it takes a great deal of expertise even when it's a very simple pattern and adds a delicacy to your knitting that lifts it above plain knitting.

Unfortunately, many people feel that lace knitting will be just too fiddly for them, especially if charts are involved, and tend to avoid patterns that have any kind of lace knitted into them, but it's really not hard when you know what you're doing – as you'll see from these socks!

This tutorial has both photos and videos to go along with the written instructions to help you. I've put the video links after the photos so you'll need to get to the end of each section to find them - and I'd recommend that you read each section first anyway before you start knitting so that you're sure you're happy with what you're doing.

Although it looks quite complicated, this lace pattern is much easier than you might expect. It's worked in blocks of 6 stitches over 4 rounds, and the 6 stitch blocks are repeated around the sock.

The lace pattern is created by knitting increases and decreases so no extra needles or special techniques are required - there's nothing in here that you probably haven't already done in other projects. What I like about this pattern is that although it's lacy, the lace sections form ribbed stripes which make it easy to see where you're up to.

They're a bit more feminine than a plain sock but aren't so floaty that you can lose your place (and your temper) when you're knitting them.

The heel is a heel flap and gusset-type heel knitted in heel stitch - just the same as the one on the Sockalong sock. I felt that there was enough going on with the rest of the sock to not want to create a "busy" heel as well.

Before we get started on knitting the sock, let's take a look at the lace pattern. I'm going to give you written and charted instructions, and don't worry if you've never read a chart before because I'll show you how to do that. Think of it as a road map to give you directions so that you can visually see where you are as well as reading instructions.

Here's the chart for the lace pattern ...

I know it looks like some kind of Battleships game but it's really not that complicated when you understand how it works!

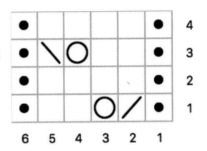

4 rows to the pattern

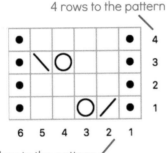

6 stitches to the pattern

Firstly, you can see that there are 4 rows (the numbers going up the right-hand side) and 6 stitches (the numbers going along the bottom).

The numbers go outwards from the first square on the bottom right hand side which is always the first stitch and that's where you'll start from, but we'll come back to that in a minute.

Here's the key for the Easy Lace Socks:

Key

☐	knit
●	purl
O	yfwd
╱	k2tog
╲	ssk

Every chart is created by showing a combination of symbols to represent each stitch. Once you can read a chart, you'll see that it's faster to do that than having to read written instructions all the time and just like using a road map when you're out and about, you need a key to tell you what each of the symbols mean.

There are some differences between symbols on patterns but for the most part they are a universal system and the pattern should always tell you what the symbols on the chart that is being used represent.

There will also usually be written instructions for how to complete each stitch if it's not a knit or purl stitch so don't worry if you don't recognise a symbol, the designer should make everything clear!

Remember I said that you always start from the bottom right hand corner? You read the chart from right to left and upwards one row at a time.

For row 2, you'll go back to the right-hand side and read along the row 2 line, and the same for row 3 and so on.

Some people like to mark off the rows as they go along so that they can see where they're up to - you can use a ruler or write on the pattern. If you're using a pattern with a chart (paid for or free) and don't want to write on your original pattern, it's OK to make a copy of the chart for your own personal use as long as you don't share it with anyone else for copyright reasons.

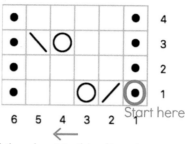

Read the chart in this direction

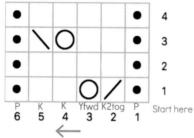

Read the chart in this direction

Using the key on the previous page to tell you which stitches to knit, you'll complete the first row of the chart like this:

You may be wondering how this 6 stitch pattern is going to work with our 60 stitch sock and that's very simple too.

If I were to write the pattern out for more than the 6 stitches it covers, it would look like this:

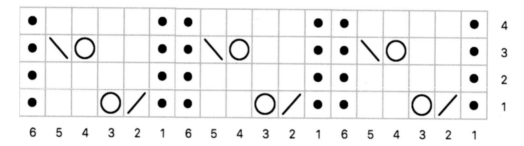

You simply repeat the pattern for the whole 60 stitches of the sock; it works in such a way that the pattern fits perfectly with 30 stitches for the front of the sock and 30 stitches for the back which makes it easy to fit in your heel flap.

Can you see how it works with the basic lace pattern? Once you've worked the first 6 stitches, you just keep repeating it until you get to the end of the round.

This is based on a 60 stitch cast on so if you cast on more or less there will need to be a change to make the stitches fit.

Have another look at the knitted pattern and you can see how the blocks fit together so that there's a purl section between each lace section. You might even be able to see how the stitches relate to the chart now, but don't worry if it all still seems like a game of Battleships, it should make sense when you start knitting.

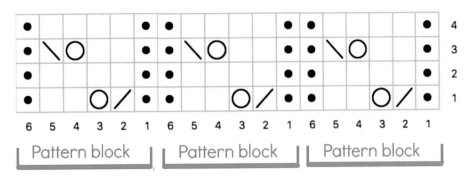

Pattern block | Pattern block | Pattern block

OK, let's take a look at how we adjust the pattern for a bigger sized sock. Because the pattern is six stitches wide, you'll find that if you increase (or decrease) the number of stitches in your sock then the pattern won't fit evenly. This isn't a problem - you can just knit or purl the extra stitches at the sides of your sock and they will look like they were always meant to be there. Let me show you:

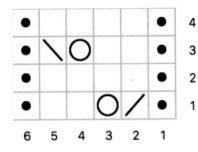

Here's the stitch pattern for 60 stitches again:

This pattern will be repeated right across each half of the sock (the front half and the back half, both of which are 30 stitches).

If you cast on 64 stitches then you'll have 32 stitches across the front and back of the sock so that will be one extra stitch on each side of the front and one extra stitch on each side of the back (a total of 4 extra stitches = 64).

You need to do something with the extra stitch at each end but you can't fit a whole pattern block in so you just need something that is in keeping with the rest of the pattern.

In this case, I've suggested that you knit the stitch so that you don't get a big block of purl stitches:

Work one knit stitch at each end of the "front" and "back" of your sock

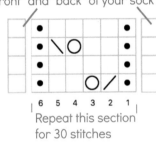

Repeat this section for 30 stitches

Work a knit and purl stitch at each end of the "front" and "back" of your sock

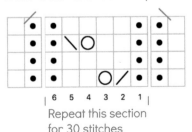

Repeat this section for 30 stitches

It's very similar for 68 stitches - this time I've added a knit and a purl stitch, but when you get to 72 stitches, you have 6 extra stitches on each side which means that you can fit another lace pattern block in on each side so it goes back to the same pattern as the 60-stitch sock.

If you want to make your sock smaller than 60 stitches you'll need to do the same thing with the pattern but in reverse so that you take out a block of the lace pattern but still do something with the stitches.

OK, I think that's everything before we get started - let the fun begin!

Easy Lace Socks

These lace socks are constructed as top down socks with a heel flap and gusset heel. The heel flap is knitted in heel stitch, which creates a durable, cushioned heel. This pattern will create a medium-sized sock but can be adjusted for other sizes.

Gauge   30 stitches to 4 inches (10 cm) in stocking stitch (worked in the round) on 2.5 mm needles

Materials

2.5 mm needles – short circular needle, DPNs (Double Pointed Needles) or an 80 cm circular for magic loop
1 x 100g skein of Doulton Flock Border Leicester 4ply in shade Cringle Moor
1 set DPNs size 3.0 mm (optional)
1 set DPNs size 2.5 mm (not required for magic loop)
Stitch markers
Wool needle

Abbreviations

K	Knit
K2tog	Knit two stitches together
P	Purl
Slip 1	Slip 1 stitch purlwise
SSK	Slip the first stitch on the left-hand needle knitwise onto the right-hand needle, slip the second stitch on the left-hand needle purlwise onto the right-hand needle, slip both stitches back onto the left-hand needle and knit together through back loop.
St(s)	Stitch(es)
yfwd	Bring the yarn forward from the back of the work between the needles to the front. When you knit the next stitch, your yarn will go over the top of the needle to create a new stitch.
( )	Repeat instructions inside brackets

Pattern notes

- It is often easier to cast on using DPNs before changing to the short circular needle and joining into the round and so this pattern has been written for this method. If you want to use magic loop you will be able to cast on with the larger circular needle if you prefer to do so, but remember not to pull your cast on stitches too tight. If you use DPNs, you might find it easiest to cast on and work 2 rows before dividing the stitches across the needles.
- Use lifelines in your work as often as you feel you need to – there's no limit to the number of them that you can use in one sock! You can find instructions for creating lifelines on page 33.
- Mark each row on your chart as you work it – it's easier to work out where you're up to if you have to put your knitting down for a while.
- If you have to take your work back, unravel one round at a time and don't forget to amend your chart so that you know where you're up to.

Pattern – make both the same

Cast on 60 [64:68:72] stitches using 3.0 mm needle.

Row 1:   (K2, P2), repeat to end, turn.
Row 2:   (K2, P2), repeat to end, turn.

Change to 2.5 mm needles. At this point, change to a short circular, magic loop or divide the stitches across DPNs and join into a circle, place marker. Continue in K2, P2 rib for 14 more rounds or until desired length of rib.

 Here's the video for the cable cast-on, transferring to a short circular and joining into the round: http://bit.ly/EasyLaceCastOn

Lace pattern

Start the lace pattern on the next round. I'm going to give you the chart instructions first and then show you how the lace is worked below. The lace pattern block is worked in sections of 6 stitches over 4 rounds.

As you can see from the key, there's nothing more complicated here than a yarn forward increase and two decreases which you've already used on other pairs of socks.

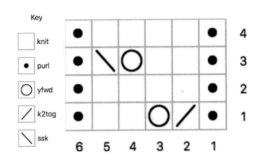

Here's how to complete that first lace block, and then when it comes to your sock you're going to pick the pattern section that fits with the size you're making - I've put those after these photos.

Round (row) 1

1 Purl the first stitch ...

2 Knit two stitches together ...

29

3 Wrap the yarn around the needle in an anti-clockwise direction, so that it's back in the right place for you to knit the next stitch ...

4 Knit two stitches ...

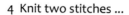

5 Purl one stitch

Round (row) 2 : Purl the purl stitches and knit the knit stitches.

Round (row) 3

1 Purl the first stitch ...

2 Knit the next two stitches ...

3 Wrap the yarn around the needle in an anti-clockwise direction so that it returns to the back of your work ready to knit the next stitch ...

4 Now you're going to do an SSK decrease so slip the first stitch knitwise from the left-hand needle to the right-hand needle ...

slip the next stitch purlwise from the left-hand needle to the right-hand needle ...

Now slip both stitches back onto the left-hand needle and knit them through the back loop ...

5 Purl the next stitch.

Round (row) 4: Purl the purl stitches and knit the knit stitches.

Here's the video for working the lace section:
http://bit.ly/CreatingLaceStitches

Here are the written and charted instructions for the lace chart - choose the size that fits with the size of sock you're making.

60 stitches

Round 1:   (P1, K2tog, yfwd, K2, P1), repeat to marker.
Round 2:   (P1, K4, P1), repeat to marker.
Round 3:   (P1, K2, yfwd, SSK, P1), repeat to marker.
Round 4:   (P1, K4, P1), repeat to marker.

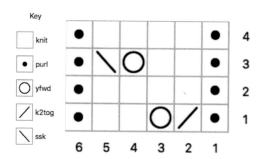

Work one knit stitch at each end of the "front" and "back" of your sock

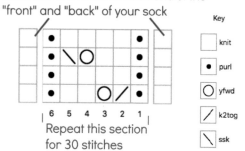

Repeat this section for 30 stitches

64 stitches

Round 1:   K1, (P1, K2tog, yfwd, K2, P1) 5 times, K2
           (P1, K2tog, yfwd, K2, P1), 5 times, K1
Round 2:   K1, (P1, K4, P1) 5 times, K2, (P1, K4, P1) 5 times, K1
Round 3:   K1, (P1, K2, yfwd, SSK, P1) 5 times, K2,
           (P1, K2, yfwd, SSK, P1) 5 times, K1
Round 4:   K1, (P1, K4, P1) 5 times, K2, (P1, K4, P1) 5 times, K1

68 stitches

Round 1:   K1, P1 (P1, K2tog, yfwd, K2, P1) 5 times, P1, K2, P1,
           (P1, K2tog, yfwd, K2, P1) 5 times, P1, K1
Round 2:   K1 P1, (P1, K4, P1) 5 times, P1, K2, P1, (P1, K4, P1) 5
           times, P1, K1
Round 3:   K1, P1, (P1, K2, yfwd, SSK, P1) 5 times, P1, K2, P1 (P1,
           K2, yfwd, SSK, P1) 5 times, P1, K1
Round 4:   K1 P1, (P1, K4, P1) 5 times, P1, K2, P1, (P1, K4, P1) 5
           times, P1 K1

Work a knit and purl stitch at each end of the "front" and "back" of your sock

Repeat this section for 30 stitches

72 stitches - As for 60 stitches.

Continue to knit each round in pattern until desired length before start of heel ending on round 4 of the pattern (for me, this is 14 repeats of the pattern giving 72 rounds in total including the rib). If you want to make the leg longer or shorter, you don't have to finish on round 4 but do make a note of which round you finish on as you'll start on the next round when you work on the gusset.

Lifelines

You may want to use a lifeline whilst you're working your lace section to give yourself some added security in case you go wrong. Have you ever seen a rock climber securing themselves to the rock they're climbing so that if they fall they will only go as far as the last place they attached themselves to? That's exactly how a lifeline works and if you've never used a lifeline in your knitting before, you're going to love them – they're not just for socks, you can use them for any project.

You'll need a strong thread or thin yarn (some people like to use dental floss but if you choose to do this, don't pick the waxed minty variety!) - I use quilting cotton because I happen to have a large reel of it - and a wool needle.

Thread your wool needle with a length of the cotton and thread it into the stitches on your needle. Try to go right through the stitch rather than catching the yarn, and take the thread right around your sock.

Once the cotton is threaded through all of the stitches, leave a long end so that it doesn't pull out again. I usually knot the two ends of the cotton together if I'm using a lifeline in a sock - it's not so easy to do that with a shawl!

There's no limit to the number of lifelines you can have; just put them in wherever you feel comfortable. This sock is one that I've been working on with a ten row lace pattern and I've put a lifeline in at the end of each pattern block.

When you've finished with the lifeline, you just pull the cotton back through the stitches, and if you need to take your knitting out at any point you can safely take the needles out of your work and pull it back without needing to unpick it one stitch at a time. The yarn won't go any further than the lifeline and you can pick the stitches up again and carry on as if nothing had gone wrong. Just like magic, eh? ☺

 Here's the lifelines video: http://bit.ly/EasyLaceLifelines

Heel Flap

Change to 2.5 mm DPNs if you are using a short circular. It is possible to knit the heel flap and gusset on the circular but it's fiddly, especially if you're using one of the really tiny circular needle sizes, so I usually swap to DPNs here. You are going to create the heel flap from half the number of stitches that you cast on, so if you have cast on more or less than 60 stitches, remember to adjust the number of stitches when you start the heel flap.

Row 1:   K2, (Slip 1, K1) until you have 30 [32:34:36] stitches on your needle, turn.
Row 2:   Slip 1, P to end, turn.
Row 3:   (Slip 1, K1) to end, turn.

Repeat rows 2 and 3 until heel flap measures approximately 2 inches (5 cm), finishing on row 3 (for me this is approx 35 rows). If you want to make the heel flap longer, continuing knitting rows 2 and 3 until you reach the desired length, but remember that you will need to pick up more stitches to create the gusset.

 Here's the heel flap video: http://bit.ly/EasyLaceHeelFlap

Turn heel

Hooray! This is the bit where the sock starts to look like a sock. Some people worry about this bit but take it slowly and you'll be fine. If you want to, put a lifeline in at the top of your heel flap so that you'll know that you can take the stitches back easily if you need to.

Row 1:   Slip 1, P16 [17:18:19], P2tog, P1, turn.
Row 2:   Slip 1, K5, SSK, K1, turn.
Row 3:   Slip 1, P6, P2tog, P1, turn.
Row 4:   Slip 1, K7, SSK, K1, turn.

Continue in this way, adding one stitch between slip stitch and SSK or P2tog on each row (ie, Row 5: Slip 1, **P8**, P2tog, P1; Row 6: Slip 1, **K9**, SSK, K1, etc) until all of the heel stitches are used. Knit across the heel stitches if required to bring you to the left-hand side of the heel flap ready to pick up 1 stitch for every 2 rows knitted.

Remember that if you made the heel flap bigger, you will need to pick up more stitches. Once you have picked up the stitches, place marker. Knit across the top of the foot stitches in pattern starting with **round 1** (or the next round if you finished on a different one), place marker, then pick up 1 stitch for every 2 rows of heel flap knitted up the other side of the heel. Knit across the top of the heel and then shape gusset as follows.

Note: If you are using DPNs and/or have placed your stitches on a stitch holder, you can arrange the needles as follows: Needle 1 for stitches across heel, Needle 2 for picked-up stitches down side of foot, Needle 3 for stitches across top of foot (knit stitches off stitch holder if required), Needle 4 for picked-up stitches on other side of foot. You may find that stitch markers are not required at first.

 Here's the video link for the heel turn: http://bit.ly/EasyLaceHeelTurn

Shape gusset

Round 1:   K to 3 sts before the marker, K2tog, K1, slip marker, knit in pattern to next marker, slip marker, K1, SSK, K to marker.

Round 2:   Slip marker, knit in pattern to next marker, slip marker, knit to 3 sts before marker.

Round 3:   K2tog, K1, slip marker, knit in pattern to next marker, slip marker, K1, SSK, K to marker.

Repeat rounds 2 and 3 to shape the gusset. Continue in this way, decreasing by two stitches at the gusset on every other row until there are 60 [64:68:72] stitches on the needle.

You can see the line of the gusset very clearly in this picture:

 Here's the video link for shaping the gusset:
http://bit.ly/EasyLaceGusset

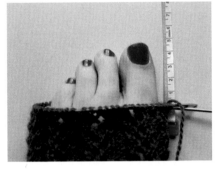 Once you have 60 [64:68:72] stitches again, continue to knit each round until you reach approximately 2 inches (5 cm) before the desired length ready to start the toes. For my size 5 feet, this is about 45 rounds. Don't be afraid to try your sock on before decreasing for the toes, and make sure that you're standing up when you measure your sock as you need your full weight on your foot. Sometimes you have to do more rounds than you think to get to where you need to be, but it's always worth making sure that your sock is the right length otherwise it will pull against your toes and also pull the heel under your foot, neither of which are very comfortable!

Toes

I've chosen to knit the toes in plain knit but if you want to continue the pattern to the decreases you can do so. At some point whilst decreasing for the toes, if you are using a short circular you may need to change to DPNs or use magic loop as the number of stitches becomes too small for the circular. It's up to you when you choose to do that, and how you distribute the stitches across the needles; just keep following the pattern as set.

Create the toes as follows:

Round 1:   K1, SSK, K24 (26:28:30)sts, K2tog, K1, place marker, K1, SSK, K24 (26:28:30) sts, K2tog, K1.
(56 [60:64:68] sts)

Round 2:   Knit one round, slipping markers as you come to them.

Round 3:   K1, SSK, K to 3 sts before marker, K2tog, K1, slip marker, K1, SSK, K to 3 sts before marker, K2tog, K1.
(52 [56:60:64] sts)

Repeat rounds 2 and 3 until you have 28 stitches left and divide these between two needles so that front and back of socks match (14 stitches on each needle).

 The video link for the toe decreases is here: http://bit.ly/EasyLaceToeDecreases

Finally, you're going to graft the toes using Kitchener stitch. Again, this is another part of the sock that people worry about but as long as you take your time and try to pick a time when you won't be disturbed then you'll be fine. If you want to see photos of how the Kitchener stitch is completed you can find them on page 112.

 The video link of how to do it is here: http://bit.ly/EasyLaceKitchener

All you need to do now is to sew the seam together where you knitted your first two rows of rib on DPNs, tightening it up if you need to, and your first sock is done. Knit another one to match and you'll soon be wearing your pair of Easy Lace Socks!

PATCHWORK SOCKS

How can you use lots of different yarns in a sock but not simply knit them into stripes? Is there a way that you can do it that will show off the yarns in bigger shapes? I pondered on this for quite some time until I realised that using intarsia meant there were no limitations!

I created this pattern to show off mini-skeins of yarn, although you could just as easily use leftovers. I like the idea that multi-coloured socks don't have to be striped or variegated and that we can create the blocks of colour for ourselves which works perfectly with the intarsia method of knitting.

Although the intarsia technique is more usually knitted flat, these socks will be knitted in the round so don't worry that there are going to be any seams to sew up. It might seem a bit fiddly at first but it's really not hard to do and there is nothing complicated that you will need to practice first.

What I really like about this patchwork pattern is that you have free reign to do whatever you like! It can feel a little odd at first to be making it up as you go along – after all, most of our knitting is done by following a pattern that's been written to create something that looks exactly the same as the pattern picture – but once you realise that you can't go wrong, it's surprisingly liberating. You can make your squares as big or as small as you want to, you can add rectangles in here and there and who's to say that anything you knitted wasn't intentional? You have permission to do your own thing!

This tutorial has both photos and videos to go along with the written instructions to help you. I've put the video links after the photos so you'll need to get to the end of each section to find them - and I'd recommend that you read each section first anyway before you start knitting so that you're sure you're happy with what you're doing.

The heel is a heel flap and gusset-type heel which you will very familiar with from other patterns that I've written. I've used a new stitch which I've called the Ribbed Heel stitch; it's a bit stretchier than the usual heel stitch so if you're someone who finds a regular heel flap a bit tight across your foot, then using this stitch should make a bit of a difference. It's super-easy, and it also works very well if you want to use it for reinforcing the soles and toes of socks too – just replace the regular heel stitch with this one.

Before we launch into the pattern, I just want to tell you about the wrap and turn technique that I've used with this sock. It's pretty much impossible to not see a join at all, but there's a trick you can do later to improve the appearance if you find that it doesn't look the way you want it to which I'll show you, and the visibility of the join does seem to work out slightly differently depending on the yarn that you choose too. I've written the pattern so that the seams are mirrored so that you can wear both the joins on the inside and then nobody will ever notice them.

Basically, all that we're going to be doing is knitting around the sock in the usual way to start off, but when we get to the end of the round, we're going to turn our sock around and work back the way we've come. That's all there is to it! It means that one round will be knit and the next will be purl, but you'll be able to pick up your colours as you come to them and there won't be any issues with yarn loops inside your socks.

If you look at this sample, you can see where the two colours meet …

When you get to the end of your round, you wrap the yarn around the next stitch and turn your work, and then when you get to that wrap on the next round, you pick it up and knit it or purl it –

that way you never notice it, although you might like the idea of leaving it as a design feature as it looks a bit like sewn stitches as in the picture on the left.

I've got plenty of photos and videos to show you how it works, but it's really not as hard as you might think!

Right then, let's get started!

Patchwork Socks

These socks are constructed as top down socks with a heel flap and gusset. The heel is knitted in ribbed heel stitch, which creates a durable, cushioned heel. The intarsia method is used for creating the patchwork squares and because the socks are knitted in the round, a wrap and turn is used which means that every other round will be a purl round.

Gauge   This pattern as written will create a medium-sized sock. The gauge is based on 7.5 stitches per inch (2.5 cm) on 2.5 mm needles knitted in the round (30 sts to 4 inches (10 cm)). To adjust the size for this sock, just add or remove stitches in blocks of 4 from the cast on total but it's always best to calculate the correct number of stitches for your foot before starting - you can find the Sock Stitch Calculation on page 9. Remember that you will need to make adjustments when turning the heel if you have more or less stitches.

Materials

2.5 mm needles – short circular needle, DPNs (Double Pointed Needles) or an 80 cm circular for magic loop.
100g of 4ply sock yarn in different colours (leftovers are perfect!) - *I used 5 x 20g mini skeins of British Stein Fine Wool 4ply from The Little Grey Sheep*
1 set double pointed needles (DPNs) size 3.0 mm (optional)
1 set double pointed needles (DPNs) size 2.5 mm (not required for magic loop)
Stitch markers
Wool needle

Abbreviations

K	Knit
K2tog	Knit two stitches together
P	Purl
P2togtbl	Purl the next two stitches together by putting your right-hand needle through the stitches from left to right at the back of the left-hand needle. As an alternative, knitting expert Barbara Walker's method of purling the next stitch on the left-hand needle, slipping the purled stitch back onto the left-hand needle and slipping the second stitch on the left-hand needle over the purled stitch can be used instead.
Slip 1	Slip 1 stitch purlwise
SSK	Slip the first stitch on the left-hand needle knitwise onto the right-hand needle, slip the second stitch on the left-hand needle purlwise onto the right-hand needle, slip both stitches back onto the left-hand needle and knit together through back loop.
St(s)	Stitch(es)
( )	Repeat the instructions inside the brackets.

Note: It is often easier to cast on using DPNs before changing to the short circular needle. If you want to use magic loop you will be able to cast on with the larger circular needle if you prefer to do so, but remember not to pull your cast on stitches too tight. If you use DPNs, you might find it easier to cast on and work 2 rows before dividing the stitches across the needles.

Pattern – make both the same

Cast on 60 stitches using 3.0 mm double pointed needles.

Row 1:   (K2, P2), repeat to end, turn.
Row 2:   (K2, P2), repeat to end, turn.

Change to 2.5 mm needles. At this point, change to a short circular, magic loop or divide the stitches across DPNs and join into a circle, place marker. Continue in K2, P2 rib for 14 more rounds or desired length of rib.

 Here's the video link for the cable cast-on, transferring to a short circular needle and joining into the round: http://bit.ly/PatchworkCastOn

Leg

I have not given charts for how you should put the patches together - simply follow the instructions below and make your patchwork socks unique! All I would say is that the more colours you use at any one time, the more risk of tangled yarn so either cut lengths of the yarn to work with or make sure you untangle them on a regular basis.

I have written these instructions to include the use of a stitch marker on the leg and foot sections, but you may find that it becomes easier not to use one as you will use the wrapped stitch as your marker. If that's the case for you, don't worry about taking the stitch marker off as you will always know where the start and end of your round is by the wrapped stitches.

Intarsia method - read this before knitting

Start the leg section by using your first new colour, join the yarn by twisting it around the cuff colour so that you don't get a hole.

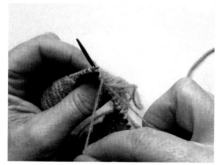

I always choose to weave the ends in by bringing the tail end of the yarn upwards over the working yarn whilst you knit the next stitch ...

and then downwards over the working yarn again when you knit the next stitch so that the tail end is firmly anchored. You can see how it works in the video (link at the end of this section).

Knit for as many stitches as you want your first patch to be, then join in a new colour, and another until you have as many yarns joined in as you would like, remembering to twist the yarns as you join them so that you don't get a hole where the colours meet. If you weave all the yarns in as you go, you should get a neat line like this on the wrong side of your work.

When you reach the end of the round, it's time to create the first wrap.

I haven't used a stitch marker in the photos as it's easier to see what I'm doing without one, but if you have one on your needle, slip it from the left needle to the right.

Then slip the first stitch after the marker to the right-hand needle ...

wrap the yarn around the stitch (not the needle) bringing it from the back of the sock to the front ...

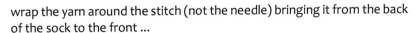

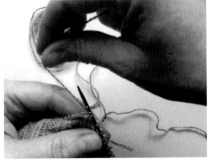

41

slip the stitch back from the right-hand needle to the left and slip the stitch marker back onto the left-hand needle and turn your sock. You are going to purl the next round so continue the wrap to bring the yarn to the front of your work then follow the instructions for all purl rounds.

Note: don't pull the yarn too tightly when you wrap the stitch – if you leave it quite loose, it's easier to adjust the stitches later so that the join is not as noticeable.

Follow these instructions for all purl rounds

Purl across all the stitches of the round, twisting the yarns as you change colours so that you don't get a hole. When you reach the wrapped stitch at the end of the round, pick up the wrapped yarn ...

and purl it together with the stitch that it was wrapped around.

Slip the stitch marker from the left-hand needle to the right-hand needle, slip the next stitch from the left-hand needle to the right-hand needle ...

wrap the yarn around the stitch (not the needle), bringing it from the front of the sock to the back ...

slip the stitch back from the right-hand needle to the left, slip the stitch marker back to the left-hand needle and turn your sock.

You are going to knit the next round so continue the wrap to bring the yarn to the back of your work, then follow the instructions for all knit rounds.

Note: don't pull the yarn too tightly when you wrap the stitch – if you leave it quite loose, it's easier to adjust the stitches later so that the join is not as noticeable.

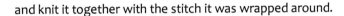

Follow these instructions for all knit rounds

Knit all the stitches until you reach the end of the round, twisting the yarns as you change colours so that you don't get a hole. When you reach the wrapped stitch at the end of the round, pick up the wrapped yarn ...

and knit it together with the stitch it was wrapped around.

Slip the stitch marker from the left needle to the right, slip the first stitch after the marker to the right-hand needle ...

wrap the yarn around the stitch (not the needle) bringing it from the back of the sock to the front and slip the stitch back from the right-hand needle to the left, slip the stitch marker back to the left-hand needle and turn your sock.

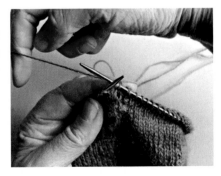

You are going to purl the next round so continue the wrap to bring the yarn to the front of your work, then follow the instructions for all purl rounds.

Note: don't pull the yarn too tightly when you wrap the stitch – if you leave it quite loose it's easier to adjust the stitches later so that the join is not as noticeable.

 Here's the video for weaving in the yarn ends and creating the wraps: http://bit.ly/PatchworkJoiningYarns

Change colours as often as you like so that your patchwork blocks show off your yarns, breaking the yarns and re-joining them according to your preference. I found that the socks look better if you make bigger patches rather than smaller ones as they can get a bit lost in the overall sock. Do be aware that your yarns will get into a tangle as you go along, so you'll need to keep untangling them. Using long lengths rather than balls can be helpful here.

Continue to knit or purl each round until you reach the desired length before the start of your heel (for me, this is about 6 inches (15 cm) - usually around 72 rounds in total including the rib).

You may find that you still need to do a bit of tidying up on the reverse side of your sock even when you weave the ends in as you go, but it's a lot less bothersome than leaving all the ends until you've finished! ☺

Heel Flap

I found it easiest to work the heel flap in one colour, but you could continue with your patchwork colours or even stripes if you wanted to - just be aware that joins in your rows on the heels could become weaker areas which may rub into a hole if you are heavy on your heels in hand-knitted socks.

Change to 2.5 mm DPNs if you are using a short circular needle. You are going to create the heel flap from half the number of stitches that you cast on, so if you have cast on more or less than 60 stitches, remember to adjust the number of stitches when you start the heel flap.

To create the heel flap on the other side of the sock so that the joins of each sock will be on different sides (ie, both on the inside or both on the outside), work 30 stitches in patchwork pattern before you start the heel flap on the second sock.

Row 1:   K2, (Slip 1, P1) until you have 28 stitches on your needle, Slip 1, K1, turn. (30 stitches)
Row 2:   Slip 1, (P1, K1) to last 3 stitches, P3, turn.
Row 3:   Slip 1, K1, (Slip 1, P1) to last 2 stitches, Slip 1, K1, turn.

Repeat rows 2 and 3 until heel measures approximately 2 inches (5 cm), finishing on row 3 (for me this is approximately 35 rows). If you want to make the heel flap longer, continue knitting rows 2 and 3 until you reach the desired length, but remember that you will need to pick up more stitches to create the gusset.

The ribbed heel stitch looks different to the regular heel stitch as it has more defined rib lines on the outside of the heel flap ...

and knit rather than purl rows on the inside.

 Here's the video for creating the heel flap:
http://bit.ly/PatchworkRibbedHeelFlap

Heel turn

I chose to work the heel turn in one colour as I thought it would be more comfortable but you can continue the patchwork colours if you want to.

Note: For a larger or smaller sock, you will need to alter the number of purl stitches in the first row of the heel (marked in bold below), increasing by 1 stitch for each block of 4 stitches extra that you cast on, or decreasing by 1 stitch for each block of 4 stitches less than 60 stitches. For example, if you cast on 64 stitches, your first row would be Slip 1, **P17**, P2tog, P1, turn.

Row 1:   Slip 1, **P16**, P2tog, P1, turn.
Row 2:   Slip 1, K5, SSK, K1, turn.
Row 3:   Slip 1, P6, P2tog, P1, turn.
Row 4:   Slip 1, K7, SSK, K1, turn.

Continue in this way, adding one stitch between slip stitch and SSK or P2tog on each row (ie, Row 5: Slip 1, **P8**, P2tog, P1; Row 6: Slip 1, **K9**, SSK, K1, etc) until all of the heel stitches are used.

 Here's the video for the heel turn: http://bit.ly/PatchworkHeelTurn

Gusset

To continue the patchwork through the gusset and down the foot, you will need to join new yarns for the gusset so it is recommended that you read through the instructions first before you start.

First, you need to decide on the colour for the sole of your foot - if you want to keep it the same as your heel, you will need to ensure that the working yarn is on the **right hand side** of your heel flap as you look at it with the outside of your heel flap facing you, otherwise you can use that yarn to pick up your first set of gusset stitches so it will need to be on the **left hand side** of your heel flap as you look at it.

You are going to pick up 1 stitch for every 2 rows knitted down the **left-hand side** of your heel flap. This will mean joining new yarn unless you have decided not to use the same colour across the heel as mentioned above, in which case you will have your working yarn at the left-hand side of your heel ready to use. Remember that if you made the heel flap bigger, you will need to pick up more stitches. Once you have picked up the stitches, place marker.

Knit across the top of the foot stitches - if you find that the yarn is at the wrong side of each block of colour, simply bring the yarn across the back of the sock so that you can use it to knit with ...

and then twisting it around the previous yarn so that you don't get a hole, knit across the first couple of stitches ...

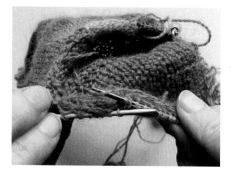

then on the next stitch, tuck your needle underneath the float loop ...

wind the yarn around and knit the stitch as usual, pulling it underneath the loop to anchor the yarn under the working yarn.

You only need to do this every few stitches as you knit so that the float won't catch on your toes as you put your sock on.

When you have worked the top of the foot stitches, place marker then pick up 1 stitch for every 2 rows of heel flap knitted up the other side of the heel. You will need to join new yarn for these stitches. Knit across the top of the heel stitches using the yarn that you used to complete your heel turn, or join a new colour if preferred. When you get to the first set of picked up stitches again, you will need to create floats as you may have done with the top of the foot stitches, anchoring the yarn with the working yarn so that the floats are not too long.

Note: If you are using DPNs and/or have placed your stitches on a stitch holder, you can arrange the needles as follows: Needle 1 for stitches across heel, Needle 2 for picked-up stitches down side of foot, Needle 3 for stitches across top of foot (knit stitches off stitch holder if required), Needle 4 for picked-up stitches on other side of foot. You may find that stitch markers are not required at first.

Shape gusset

Gusset decreases - read this first: When you reach the decreases for the gusset, you'll create the K2tog decrease just as you would do for any other sock, but as you're working backwards and forwards around your sock, you'll need to do a purl decrease when you're on the purl side. Purling two stitches together won't give you the right effect so the technique used is to purl two stitches together through the back loop.

You can either do this by taking your needle behind your stitches and putting it into the first two stitches on the needle from left to right ...

and then purling them together.

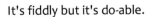

It's fiddly but it's do-able.

Or, you can use knitting expert Barbara Walker's method of purling the next stitch on the left-hand needle and transferring it back to the right-hand needle ...

Then lift the second stitch on the left-hand needle and pass it over the stitch that you just purled and put back onto the left-hand needle ...

and that will give you the same effect - and you're not contorting your hands to do it!

Create the gusset as follows:

Round 1:   K to 3 sts before the end of the first set of picked up stitches, K2tog, K1, wrap yarn around next stitch and turn. Purl back along the stitches until 3 stitches before next marker, P2togtbl, P1, purl across top of foot stitches to wrapped stitch, pick up wrap and purl stitch, turn.
Round 2:   Knit in pattern to next marker, slip marker, knit to 3 sts before marker.
Round 3:   K2tog, K1, wrap yarn around next stitch and turn. Purl back along the stitches until 3 stitches before next marker, P2togtbl, P1, purl across top of foot stitches to wrapped stitch, pick up wrap and purl stitch, turn.

Repeat rounds 2 and 3 to shape the gusset. Continue in this way, decreasing by two stitches at the gusset on every other row until there are 60 stitches on the needle. If you want to take your markers out because you can use the join line as your marker instead, you can do this now.

You can see the line of the gusset very clearly in this picture:

 Here's the video for the gusset: http://bit.ly/PatchworkGusset

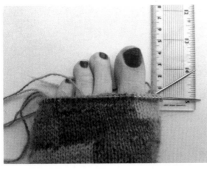

Once you have 60 stitches again, continue to knit and purl each round in your patchwork pattern until you reach approximately 2 inches (5 cm) before the desired length ready to start the toes. For my size 5 feet, this is about 45 rounds.

Don't be afraid to try your sock on before decreasing for the toes and make sure that you're standing up as you need your full weight on your foot. Sometimes you have to work more rounds than you think to get to where you need to be, but it's always worth doing that so that sock is the right length - otherwise it will pull against your toes and under your heel which isn't very comfortable!

Toes

I've chosen to knit the toes in one colour but you can continue the patchwork pattern if you want to - just be aware that the joins between the colours might become a weak spot for pokey toes! At some point whilst decreasing for the toes, if you are using a short circular needle you may need to change to DPNs or use magic loop as the number of stitches becomes too small for the circular. It's up to you when you choose to do that, and how you distribute the stitches across the needles; just keep following the pattern as set below. If you have cast on more or less than 60 stitches, you will need to adjust the number of stitches between the decreases to accommodate this.

Knit one round in the colour you want your toes to be, cutting the yarns and weaving the ends in as you go, then create the toes as follows:

Round 1:   K1, SSK, K for 24 stitches, K2tog, K1, place marker, K1, SSK, K for 24 stitches, K2tog, K1
Round 2:   Knit one round, slipping markers as you come to them
Round 3:   K1, SSK, K to 3 stitches before marker, K2tog, K1, place marker, K1, SSK, K to 3 stitches before
             marker, K2tog, K1

Repeat rounds 2 and 3 until you have 28 stitches left and divide these between two needles so that the front and back of the socks match (14 stitches on each needle).

 The video link for the toe decreases is here: http://bit.ly/PatchworkToeDecreases

Finally, you're going to graft the toes using Kitchener stitch so that you don't get a seam. This is part of the sock that does worry some people, but as long as you take your time and you choose to do it when you won't be disturbed, you'll be absolutely fine. There is a separate section on grafting the toes with Kitchener stitch on page 112.

 You can find the video on grafting the toes here: http://bit.ly/PatchworkKitchener

If you find that the join is a bit loose like this one ...

you'll find that you can tighten the stitches up by taking a wool needle and wiggling the stitches. This is why you kept the wrap quite loose; it allows you to re-align the stitches and you'll find that washing your sock will adjust the stitches too.

This is what mine looks like after I've done a bit of stitch-wiggling. Much better!

You're all done! You've just got to sew up the gap between the first two rows when you cast on, tidy up any loose ends inside your sock and then you can admire it - but not for too long as you've got a second one to cast on!

EASY COLOURWORK SOCKS

It's always a joy for me to see patterns that use more than one colour of yarn, and it's not as hard as you think to get the effect. All styles of colourwork knitting, whether classed as "stranded colourwork," "Shetland", "Fair Isle" or another name are created in the same way with more than one ball of yarn being worked at the same time.

This tutorial has both photos and videos to go along with the written instructions to help you. I've put the video links after the photos so you'll need to get to the end of each section to find them - and I'd recommend that you read each section first anyway before you start knitting so that you're sure you're happy with what you're doing.

I created this pattern with the intention of helping you to get started with colourwork so I've kept it very simple: just two colours and easy geometric shapes which will have you whizzing along in no time. We're going to tackle the pattern one row at a time and you'll see that it's easier than you think to create beautiful socks with more than one colour of yarn.

I've been able to get two pairs of socks out of the yarn that I've used and it's been interesting to see how the pattern looks different when you change the contrast.

The heel is a heel flap and gusset heel using heel stitch which you'll be familiar with from the other patterns that I've written. If you want to swap it for the slightly stretchier Ribbed Heel Stitch heel flap, have a look at the tutorial for the Patchwork Socks on page 37 as you'll find the instructions there. It doesn't use any more stitches than this heel flap so you can easily swap it without needing to make any other changes.

There are a couple of techniques with colourwork knitting that I want to show you, but I think the easiest way to do that is as we work our way through the pattern, so we'll just get started.

Easy Colourwork Socks

These socks are constructed as top down socks with a heel flap and gusset. The heel is knitted in heel stitch, which creates a durable, cushioned heel.

Size   To fit ball of foot circumference 8 [8.5:9:9.5] inches; 20 [22:23:24] cm

Gauge   30 stitches to 4 inches (10 cm) in stocking stitch (worked in the round) on 2.5 mm needles

Materials

2.5 mm needles - short circular needle, DPNs (Double Pointed Needles) or an 80 cm circular needle for magic loop
100g of 4ply sock yarn in two colours (leftovers are perfect as a contrast!) - *I used 2 x 100g skeins of Freehold Yarn Co Autumn 4ply yarn in shades Maple (main colour - MC) and Cloud (contrast colour - CC)*
1 set DPNs size 3.0 mm (optional)
1 set DPNs size 2.5 mm (not required for magic loop)
Stitch markers
Wool needle

Abbreviations

K	Knit
K2tog	Knit two stitches together
P	Purl
Slip 1	Slip 1 stitch purlwise
SSK	Slip the first stitch on the left hand needle knitwise onto the right hand needle, slip the second stitch on the left hand needle purlwise onto the right hand needle, slip both stitches back onto the left hand needle and knit together through back loop
St(s)	Stitch(es)
( )	Repeat the instructions inside the brackets

Pattern notes

- It is often easier to cast on using DPNs before changing to the short circular needle and joining into the round and so this pattern has been written for this method. If you want to use magic loop you will be able to cast on with the larger circular needle if you prefer to do so, but remember not to pull your cast on stitches too tight. If you use DPNs, you might find it easiest to cast on and work 2 rows before dividing the stitches across the needles.
- Use lifelines in your work as often as you feel you need to – there's no limit to the number of them that you can use in one sock! You can find instructions for creating lifelines on page 33.
- Mark each row on your chart as you work it – it's easier to work out where you're up to if you have to put your knitting down for a while.

- If you have to take your work back, unravel one round at a time and don't forget to amend your chart so that you know where you're up to.

Pattern – make both the same

Using MC, cast on 60 [64:68:72] stitches using 3.0 mm double pointed needles.

Row 1:   (K2, P2), repeat to end, turn.
Row 2:   (K2, P2), repeat to end, turn.

Change to 2.5 mm needles. At this point, change to a short circular needle, magic loop or divide the stitches evenly across DPNs and join into a circle; place marker. Work two more rounds of K2, P2 rib.

We're now going to do something called a **bipless rib,** but feel free to knit the rib in your usual style if you prefer. When you knit a rib section with more than one colour, you can see the colour change from the other side when you knit the purl stitches, but there's a way of stopping that. In this photo, you can see that the bottom stripe is knitted in the usual way with K2, P2 stitches on every round, but the top stripe doesn't have those "bips" in between the ribs.

This is how you do it:

Round 5:   Change to CC and knit one round.
Round 6:   (K2, P2), repeat to end.
Round 7:   Change to MC and knit one round.
Round 8:   (K2, P2) repeat to end.

The way to stop the bips is to knit all the stitches of the first colour change round, then go back to K2, P2 rib for the second round. If you look closely, you can see that the top band looks slightly narrower than the bottom one, but now you have a choice between that and the bips appearing in the wider band.

Continue in K2, P2 rib for 8 more rounds or until desired length of rib (I knit 16 rounds of rib).

 The video for working the cast on, joining into the round, bipless rib and jogless stripe (next section) is here: http://bit.ly/EasyColourworkCastOn

Leg

Using MC and the correct chart for your size, read the chart from right to left and knit rounds 1-37 changing colours where directed, then knit each round until you reach the desired length before start of heel (for me, this is usually around 72 rounds in total including the rib). If you need a reminder of how to read a chart, you can find that in the Easy Cable Socks tutorial on page 12.

There's another technique that I want to show you before you start – the **jogless stripe.**

When you knit colourwork in the round you get a "jog" when you change colours. They happen because each round is stacked on top of the previous one, but there are methods you can use to try to lessen the impact of the stripes.

The one that I use is to knit the first round of the new colour, then pick up the first stitch of the previous colour ...

put it onto the left hand needle and knit it together with the first stitch of the new colour round.

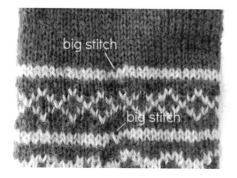

What happens now is that you get a big stitch of the contrast colour which makes the join less obvious as it hides the first stitch of the new colour. The stitch itself isn't hugely noticeable so don't worry that it will look odd!

If you look at this photo, you can see that I forgot to lift the stitch on the right hand sock on the bottom stripe – there's quite a difference so it's worth the effort!

Let's also have a look at how you're going to work your two colours at once. There's absolutely nothing wrong with picking each colour up individually whenever you need to use it, but there are other ways to hold your yarn too which do make it faster to knit colourwork. I used to knit lots of colourwork jumper samples for my local yarn shop when I was much younger and I wish I'd thought to knit like this then!

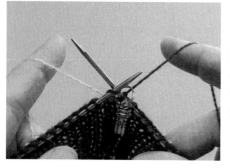

I'm an English-style knitter so I hold my working yarn in my right hand. Here, I've got my contrast colour in my left hand held in continental style. I've chosen to do this so that I can remember which is the dominant colour of the two that I'm working with, but more of that in a minute.

Whenever I need to knit with the contrast colour, I scoop the yarn from my left hand ...

and then when I need to knit the main colour, I knit as usual with my right hand. It takes a bit of practice but it's so much faster than dropping the yarns each time. You can also hold both yarns in your left or right hand – there's no "right way" to do this so experiment to see what feels right for you.

This is what the yarns look like on the wrong side. Because I'm only knitting with the contrast colour every few stitches, I get long threads called "floats" which are carried along the back of the work. It's really important not to pull the floats tight when you're working or you'll lose the stretch in your knitting and won't be able to get your sock (jumper, cardigan) on later.

I mentioned **dominant colour** and you'll be pleased to know that's a really easy concept to get your head around. When you knit with more than one colour, you'll find that you have one yarn that is on the top and the other will come from underneath. It's something that you need to pay attention to because basically, the yarn that you want to stand out in your knitting - that is, the contrast yarn - is the dominant colour and you need to make sure that the yarn is always coming from underneath the main colour. This is because it uses slightly more yarn which produces a bigger stitch and therefore makes that colour stand out more. Easy, eh? This is what your sock will look like on the inside.

The pattern would look different if the red was the dominant colour, so turning your work inside out on a regular basis to check that your pattern remains the same is a good way to make sure that you haven't swapped the dominant colour by mistake.

Finally, let's talk about what happens to those floats if they get too long. I don't recommend that you carry your floats over any more than 4 stitches with a sock or you might risk getting your toes stuck in them when you put them on. Sometimes you need to carry the contrast yarn along and is how I do it.

Start by lifting the contrast yarn over the main colour working yarn ...

then knit the next stitch with the main colour ...

then take the contrast yarn back down over the main colour working yarn again as you knit the next stitch. This will ensure that your contrast yarn remains in the right place to come up from underneath the main colour and maintain the dominance.

I hope that didn't seem too complicated! I'm sure you'll find it all quite easy once you get going!

 The video tutorial for working the colourwork section is here: http://bit.ly/EasyColourworkColours

Heel Flap

Change to 2.5 mm DPNs if you are using a short circular needle. There is no need to use DPNs if you are using magic loop. You may prefer to place the spare stitches from the top of the foot onto a stitch holder if you are using a short circular or DPNs whilst you work the heel. To create the heel flap on the other side of the sock so that the joins of each sock will be on different sides (ie, both on the inside or both on the outside), work 30 stitches (or half the number of cast on stitches for a bigger/smaller sock) before you start the flap on the second sock.

Row 1:   K2, (Slip 1, K1) until you have 30 [32:34:36] stitches on your needle, turn.
Row 2:   Slip 1, P to end, turn.
Row 3:   (Slip 1, K1) to end, turn.

Repeat rows 2 and 3 until heel flap measures approximately 2 inches (5 cm), finishing on row 3 (for me this is approx 35 rows). If you want to make the heel flap longer, continue knitting rows 2 and 3 until you reach the desired length, but remember that you will need to pick up more stitches to create the gusset.

 Here's the video for the heel flap: http://bit.ly/EasyColourworkHeelFlap

Heel turn

Row 1:   Slip 1, P16 [17:18:19], P2tog, P1, turn.
Row 2:   Slip 1, K5, SSK, K1, turn.
Row 3:   Slip 1, P6, P2tog, P1, turn.
Row 4:   Slip 1, K7, SSK, K1, turn.

Continue in this way, adding one stitch between slip stitch and SSK or P2tog on each row (ie, Row 5: Slip 1, **P8**, P2tog, P1; Row 6: Slip 1, **K9**, SSK, K1, etc) until all of the heel stitches are used.

 Here's the video for the heel turn: http://bit.ly/EasyColourworkHeelTurn

Gusset

Knit across heel stitches if required to bring you to the left hand side of the heel flap (with the outside of the flap facing you) ready to pick up 1 stitch for every 2 rows knitted. Remember that if you made the heel flap bigger, you will need to pick up more stitches. Once you have picked up the stitches, place marker. Knit across the top of the foot stitches, place marker, then pick up 1 stitch for every 2 rows of heel flap knitted up the other side of the heel. Knit across the top of the heel and then shape gusset as below.

Note: If you are using DPNs and/or have placed your stitches on a stitch holder, you can arrange the needles as follows: Needle 1 for stitches across heel, Needle 2 for picked-up stitches down side of foot, Needle 3 for stitches across top of foot (knit stitches off stitch holder if required), Needle 4 for picked-up stitches on other side of foot. You may find that stitch markers are not required at first.

If you would prefer to omit the contrast stripe, use MC throughout the gusset. To create the stripe, you are going to knit two rounds of CC, starting part-way through round 1 and finishing part-way through round 3. I have chosen to join the yarn at this point to make the join less visible, but you can join the yarn elsewhere if you choose.

Round 1:   K to 3 sts before the marker, K2tog, K1, slip marker, knit to next marker, slip marker, K1, SSK, K to start of first set of picked up stitches and join CC. Knit to marker.
Round 2:   Slip marker, knit to next marker, slip marker, knit to 3 sts before marker.
Round 3:   K2tog, K1, slip marker, knit to next marker, slip marker, K1, SSK, K start of CC round and rejoin MC. Knit to marker.

Working in MC for 2 rounds then CC for 2 rounds then back to MC for remainder of gusset, repeat rounds 2 and 3 to shape the gusset. Continue in this way, decreasing by two stitches at the gusset on every other round until there are 60 [64:68:72] stitches on the needle.

You can see the line of the gusset very clearly in this picture.

 Here's the video for the gusset:
http://bit.ly/EasyColourworkGusset

If you wish to add the next set of stripes, join in CC at approximately 2 ¾ inches (7 cm) before the desired length of your sock and knit 2 rounds CC, 2 rounds MC, 2 rounds CC and 2 rounds MC. Continue to knit each round in MC until you reach approximately 2 inches (5 cm) before the desired length ready to start the toes. For my size 5 feet, this is about 45 rounds. Don't be afraid to try your sock on before decreasing for the toes and make sure that you're standing up as you need your full weight on your foot. Sometimes you have to work more rounds than you think to get to where you need to be, but it's always worth doing that so that sock is the right length - otherwise it will pull against your toes and under your heel which isn't very comfortable!

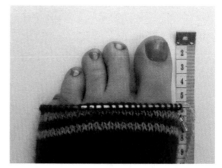

Toes

At some point whilst decreasing for the toes, if you are using a short circular you may need to change to DPNs or use magic loop as the number of stitches becomes too small for the circular. It's up to you when you choose to do that, and how you distribute the stitches across the needles; just keep following the pattern as set below. Join CC and create the toes as follows:

Round 1:   K1, SSK, K24 [26:28:30] sts, K2tog, K1, place marker, K1, SSK, K24 [26:28:30] sts, K2tog, K1.
(56 [60:64:68] sts)

Round 2:   Knit one round, slipping markers as you come to them.

Round 3:   K1, SSK, K to 3 sts before marker, K2tog, K1, slip marker, K1, SSK, K to 3 sts before marker, K2tog, K1.
(52 [56:60:64] sts)

Repeat rounds 2 and 3 until you have 28 stitches left and divide these between two needles so that front and back of socks match.

 The video for the toe decreases is here: http://bit.ly/EasyColourworkToeDecreases

Finally, you're going to graft the toes using Kitchener stitch so that you don't get a seam. This is part of the sock that does worry some people, but as long as you take your time and you choose to do it when you won't be disturbed, you'll be absolutely fine. There is a separate section on grafting the toes with Kitchener stitch on page 112

 and there's a video here:
http://bit.ly/EasyColourworkKitchener

You're all done! You've just got to sew up the gap between the first two rows when you cast on, tidy up any loose ends inside your sock and then you can admire it - but not for too long as you've got a second one to cast on!

Charts

60 stitches

Key

 Main colour

■ Contrast colour

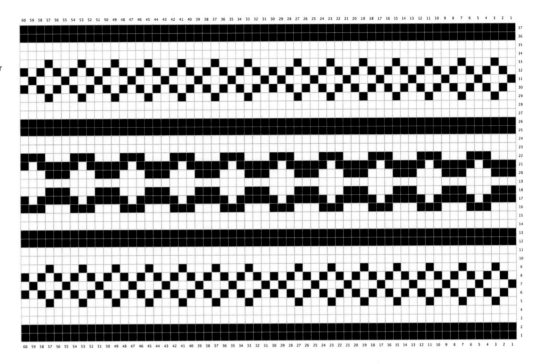

64 stitches

Key

□ Main colour

■ Contrast colour

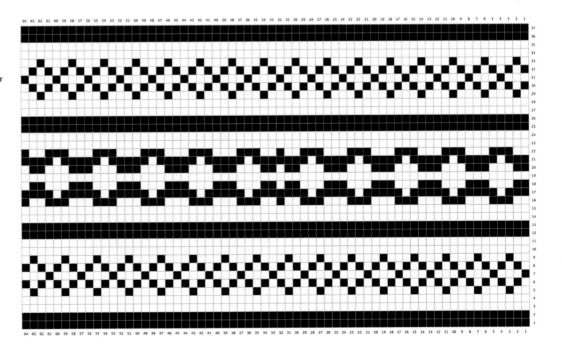

68 stitches

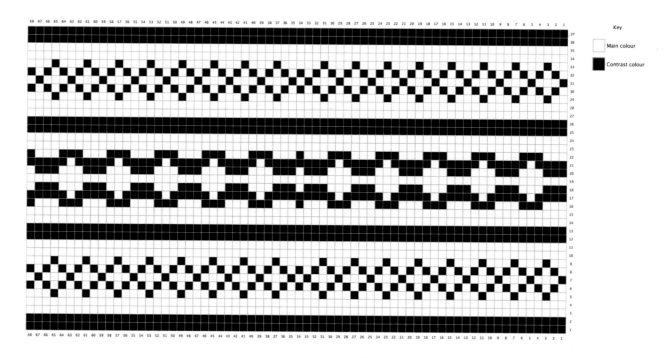

72 stitches

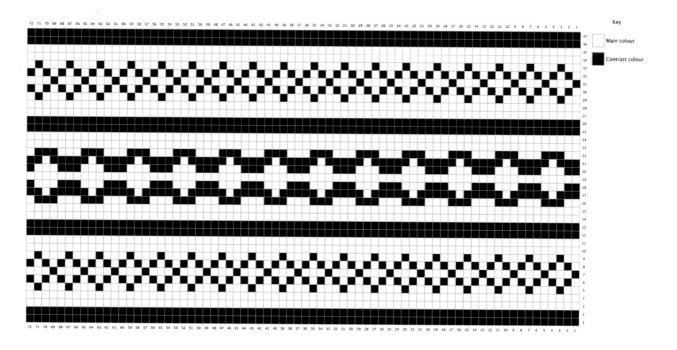

ADDITIONAL PATTERNS

Drunken Cable Socks – page 62

Beatrice Socks – page 87

Flow Through Socks – page 98

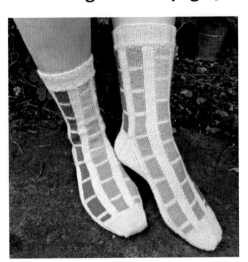

Rainbow Zig Zag Socks – page 105

These patterns are designed to use the skills that you learnt in the previous tutorials. Although I've included pictures to illustrate various points, the instructions are not as in-depth as for the previous patterns – this is quite deliberate as when you move on to other patterns, they will be written in a much more concise way. I want you to be able to tackle them with confidence so by having to think more about what you're doing with these patterns, you'll be all set by the time you're ready to cast on a new sock!

If you get stuck with these patterns, you can use the videos and the photos from the previous tutorials to help you as the process for creating the socks will be the same.

DRUNKEN CABLE SOCKS

Three drunken cables wending their weary way home … Oh dear! These cables look a bit worse for wear, weaving about the sock and unable to stand up straight on their own. I'm sure they've had a lovely time!

I love the idea that cables don't need to look formal and these ones certainly don't! Increase and decrease stitches push and pull the cables in different directions; there's nothing complicated about this pattern but you do have to follow the chart or written instructions closely so that your cables behave. These socks are constructed as top down socks with a heel flap and gusset. The heel is knitted in heel stitch, which gives a comfortable, durable heel.

This pattern is for a medium sized sock, with larger sizes suitable for men and women given in parentheses. The length of the sock is easily adjusted for any foot. There are LOTS of charts and written instructions for this pattern so do take care when you're knitting that you don't get mixed up!

The Drunken Cable Socks pattern works in exactly the same way as the Easy Cable Socks on page 12, so if you were confident in knitting the Easy Cable Socks then you'll have no trouble with this pattern, despite the charts being much bigger and looking more complicated. Have another look at the Easy Cable Socks tutorial if you need a reminder on how to read a chart – don't forget that you're always working from right to left and you're also only working one round at a time so as long as you mark off on your pattern where you're up to (it's fine to make a copy for your own personal use if you'd like to) then you won't get lost.

There are cables in the cuffs of these socks which means you'll get started on them straight away – remember to use lifelines if you need to (page 33) and also remember that there is a left and a right foot to this pattern so be sure that you're following the right one!

The cables are slightly different to the ones in the Easy Cable Socks so let's take a look at how we're going to knit those.

C3B is exactly as it says – Cable 3 Back. This tells you that you're working a cable stitch, you're going to use 3 stitches and you're going to take the stitch on your cable needle to the back of your work.

Start by slipping the first stitch of your cable block from the left hand needle onto your cable needle and hold it at the back of your work.

Next, knit the next two stitches of the cable block onto your right hand needle …

And then knit the stitch off the cable needle onto the right hand needle.

That's it! That's all there is to it! Easy, eh?

C3F works in a very similar way. It's a cable stitch using 3 stitches and you're going to take the stitches on your cable needle to the front of your work.

Slip the first two stitches of the cable block from the left hand needle onto your cable needle and hold it at the front of your work.

Knit the next stitch of the cable block onto your right hand needle …

Then knit the two stitches off the cable needle onto the right hand needle.

Another cable done!

<u>**Size**</u>   To fit ball of foot circumference 8 [8.5:9:9.5] inches; 20 [22:23:24] cm

Cables will pull the fabric of the sock in slightly so I have increased the number of stitches for each size to compensate. If you normally cast on 60 stitches, you will cast on 64; if you normally cast on 64, you will cast on 68 and so on.

<u>**Gauge**</u>   30 stitches to 4 inches (10 cm) in stocking stitch (worked in the round) on 2.5 mm needles

<u>Materials</u>

2.5 mm needles – short circular needle, DPNs (Double Pointed Needles) or 80 cm circular for magic loop
1 x 100g skein of Baa Ram Ewe Titus 4ply in shade Aire
1 set DPNs size 3.0 mm (optional)
1 set DPNs size 2.5 mm (not required for magic loop)
Stitch holder (optional)
Stitch markers
Cable needle
Wool needle

<u>Abbreviations</u>

C3B	Slip the next stitch on the left hand needle onto a cable needle and hold at the back of your work. Knit the next two stitches on the left hand needle then knit the stitch from the cable needle.
C3F	Slip the next two stitches on the left hand needle onto a cable needle and hold at the front of your work. Knit the next stitch on the left hand needle then knit the two stitches from the cable needle.
K	Knit
K2tog	Knit two stitches together
M1L	Insert the right hand needle from front to back into the bar lying between the next two stitches and slide it onto the left hand needle. Knit into the back of this new stitch.
M1R	Insert the right hand needle from back to front into the bar lying between the next two stitches and slide it onto the left hand needle. Knit into the front of this new stitch.
P	Purl
Slip 1	Slip 1 stitch purlwise
SSK	Slip the first stitch on the left hand needle knitwise onto the right hand needle, slip the second stitch on the left hand needle purlwise onto the right hand needle, slip both stitches back onto the left hand needle and Knit together through back loop
St(s)	Stitch(es)
( )	Repeat instructions inside brackets

<u>Pattern Notes</u>

- It is often easier to cast on using DPNs before changing to the short circular needle and joining into the round and so this pattern has been written for this method. If you want to use magic loop you will be able to cast on with the larger circular needle if you prefer to do so, but remember not to pull your cast on stitches too tight.

If you use DPNs, you might find it easiest to cast on and work 2 rows before dividing the stitches across the needles.

- Use lifelines in your work as often as you feel you need to – there's no limit to the number of them that you can use in one sock! You can find instructions for creating lifelines on page 33.
- Mark each row on your chart as you work it – it's easier to work out where you're up to if you have to put your knitting down for a while.
- If you have to take your work back, unravel one round at a time and don't forget to amend your chart so that you know where you're up to.

Left foot

Cast on 64 [68:72:76] stitches using 3.0 mm double pointed needles. Remember that you will need to work the chart stitches twice. **The pattern has been written for a cast on with straight needles – if you want to join straight into the round, work round 1 twice and omit round 2 of the cuff pattern.**

Using the correct cuff pattern for your size:

Row 1:   Work round 1 of cuff using chart (reading right to left) or written instructions, turn.
Row 2:   Work round 2 of cuff using chart (reading left to right) or written instructions, turn.

Change to a 2.5 mm short circular needle, magic loop or divide the stitches across DPNs and join into a circle, place marker. You might find it helps to place a second marker to indicate where the chart repeats. You will sew up the small gap where you knitted the first two rows later.

Continue to work cuff using chart for left foot (reading from right to left) or written instructions for 14 more rounds.

64 stitches (32 stitches twice)

Round 1:   P2, K2, P1, K3, P1, K1, (P2, K2, P1, K3, P1, K2) twice. (32 sts)
Round 2:   K2, P2, K1, P3, K1, P1, (K2, P2, K1, P3, K1, P2) twice.
Round 3:   P2, K2, P1, C3B, P1, K1, P2, K2, P1, K3, P1, K2, P2, K2, P1, C3B, P1, K2.
Round 4:   P2, K2, P1, K3, P1, K1, P2, K2, P1, C3B, P1, K2, P2, K2, P1, K3, P1, K2.
Round 5:   Repeat round 1.
Round 6:   Repeat round 1.
Round 7:   Repeat round 3.
Round 8:   Repeat round 1.
Round 9:   Repeat round 4.
Rounds 10-13:   Repeat rounds 6 - 9.
Round 14:   Repeat round 1.
Round 15:   Repeat round 3.
Round 16:   Repeat round 1.

68 stitches (34 stitches twice)

Round 1:	P2, K2, P1, K3, P1, K2, P2, K2, (P1, K3) twice, P2, K2, P1, K3, P1, K2. (34 sts)
Round 2:	K2, P2, K1, P3, K1, P2, K2, P2, K1, P3, (K2, P2) twice, K1, P3, K1, P2.
Round 3:	P2, K2, P1, C3B, P1, K2, P2, K2, P1, K3, (P2, K2) twice, P1, C3B, P1, K2.
Round 4:	P2, K2, P1, K3, P1, K2, P2, K2, P1, C3F, (P2, K2) twice, P1, K3, P1, K2.
Round 5:	P2, K2, P1, K3, P1, K2, P2, K2, P1, K3, (P2, K2) twice, P1, K3, P1, K2.
Round 6:	Repeat round 5.
Round 7:	Repeat round 3.
Round 8:	Repeat round 5.
Round 9:	Repeat round 4.
Rounds 10-13:	Repeat rounds 6 - 9.
Round 14:	Repeat round 5.
Round 15:	Repeat round 3.
Round 16:	Repeat round 5.

72 stitches (36 stitches twice)

Round 1:	P2, K2, (P1, K3) twice, P2, K2, P1, K3, P1, K4, P2, K2, P1, K3, P1, K2. (36 sts)
Round 2:	(K2, P2, K1, P3, K2, P2) twice, K2, P2, K2, P3, K1, P2.
Round 3:	P2, K2, P1, C3B, (P2, K2) twice, P1, K3, (P2, K2) twice, P2, C3B, P1, K2.
Round 4:	P2, K2, P1, K3, (P2, K2) twice, P1, C3F, (P2, K2) twice, P2, K3, P1, K2.
Round 5:	(P2, K2, P1, K3, P2, K2) twice, P2, K2, P2, K3, P1, K2.
Round 6:	Repeat round 5.
Round 7:	Repeat round 3.
Round 8:	Repeat round 5.
Round 9:	Repeat round 4.
Rounds 10-13:	Repeat rounds 6 - 9.
Round 14:	Repeat round 5.
Round 15:	Repeat round 3.
Round 16:	Repeat round 5.

76 stitches (38 stitches twice)

Round 1:	K2, (P2, K1, P1, K3, P1, K1, P2, K1) twice, P2, K1, P2, K3, P1, K1, P2. (38 sts)
Round 2:	P2, (K2, P1, K1, P3, K1, P1, K2, P1) twice, K2, P1, K2, P3, K1, P1, K2.
Round 3:	K2, P2, K1, P1, C3B, P1, (K1, P2) twice, K1, P1, K3, P1, (K1, P2) 3 times, C3B, P1, K1, P2.
Round 4:	K2, P2, K1, P1, K3, P1, (K1, P2) twice, K1, P1, C3F, P1, (K1, P2) 3 times, K3, P1, K1, P2.
Round 5:	Repeat round 1.
Round 6:	Repeat round 1.
Round 7:	Repeat round 3.
Round 8:	Repeat round 1.
Round 9:	Repeat round 4.
Rounds 10-13:	Repeat rounds 6 - 9.

Round 14:	Repeat round 1.
Round 15:	Repeat round 3.
Round 16:	Repeat round 1.

Working the increases in the leg section

The cables push and pull in different directions thanks to increase and decrease stitches. The decreases are SSK and K2tog decreases which should already be familiar to you from other sock patterns (they're used in the gusset) but if you need a reminder, you can look them up in the *Winwick Mum* Sockalong online tutorials or in *Super Socks*.

The increases are made using M1 (make 1) increases which lean either left or right depending on which way the cable is leaning. Using a **M1L** (make 1 left) or **M1R** (make 1 right) increase rather than the same one for each increase is neater and makes the increase less obvious in your finished sock.

Let's have a look at how the **M1L** increases are created:

Start by slipping the right hand needle underneath the bar between the last stitch on the right hand needle and the first stitch on the left hand needle …

Pick up the bar and put it on the left hand needle so that the right hand leg of the stitch is over the front of the needle towards you …

Then knit into the **back** of the stitch and that will create your new stitch.

As long as you remember to put the bar onto your needle as in the photo and knit into the back of it, you won't get a hole where you've made the new stitch.

Now let's have a look at how to create the **M1R** increase.

Slip the right hand needle underneath the bar between the last stitch on the right hand needle and the first stitch on the left hand needle, just as you did for the M1L increase ...

Pick up the bar and put it on the left hand needle so that the right hand leg of the stitch is over the back of the needle away from you ...

And then knit into the **front** of the stitch and that will create your new stitch.

As long as you remember to put the bar onto your needle as in the photo and knit into the front of it, you won't get a hole where you've made the new stitch.

You can see in this picture where the increases and decreases have dictated the direction of the cables, but because of the type of increases used, there aren't any holes.

Left Leg

Using either the charts or the written pattern for the left leg, continue to knit each round until leg measures 6 [7] inches; 15 [17] cm or desired length from cast on edge, remembering which round of the pattern you finished on for the heel flap as you will need this later. Work the chart stitches twice.

64 stitches (32 stitches twice)

Round 1:	K4, P1, K3, P1, K5, P1, C3B, P1, K6, P1, K3, P1, K2. (32 sts)
Round 2:	K4, M1L, P1, K3, P1, SSK, (K3, P1) twice, K6, P1, K3, P1, K2.
Round 3:	K5, P1, K3, P1, K2, K2tog, P1, K3, P1, M1R, K6, P1, K3, P1, K2.
Round 4:	K5, P1, C3F, (P1, K3) twice, P1, K7, P1, C3B, P1, K2.
Round 5:	K5, (P1, K3) twice, P1, C3B, P1, K7, P1, K3, P1, K2.
Round 6:	K5, (P1, K3) 3 times, P1, K5, K2tog, P1, K3, P1, M1R, K2.
Round 7:	K5, P1, K3, P1, K1, K2tog, P1, K3, P1, K7, (P1, K3) twice.
Round 8:	K5, P1, C3B, P1, K2, P1, K3, P1, K7, P1, C3B, P1, K3.
Round 9:	K5, P1, K3, P1, K2, P1, C3B, P1, K7, (P1, K3) twice.
Round 10:	K3, K2tog, P1, K3, P1, M1R, K2, P1, K3, P1, K5, K2tog, P1, K3, P1, M1R, K3.
Round 11:	K4, P1, K3, P1, K1, K2tog, P1, K3, P1, M1R, K6, P1, K3, P1, K4.
Round 12:	K4, P1, C3B, P1, K2, P1, K3, P1, K7, P1, C3B, P1, K4.
Round 13:	K4, P1, K3, P1, K2, P1, C3B, P1, K7, P1, K3, P1, K4.
Round 14:	K2, K2tog, P1, K3, P1, M1R, K2, P1, K3, P1, K5, K2tog, P1, K3, P1, M1R, K4.
Round 15:	(K3, P1) 4 times, K6, P1, K3, P1, K5.
Round 16:	K3, P1, C3B, (P1, K3) twice, P1, K6, P1, C3B, P1, K5.
Round 17:	(K3, P1) 3 times, C3F, P1, K6, P1, K3, P1, K5.
Round 18:	K1, K2tog, P1, K3, P1, M1R, (K3, P1) twice, K4, K2tog, P1, K3, P1, M1R, K5.
Round 19:	K2, P1, K3, P1, K4, M1L, K4, P1, SSK, (K3, P1) twice, K6.
Round 20:	K2, P1, C3B, P1, K5, P1, K3, P1, K4, P1, C3B, P1, K6.
Round 21:	K2, P1, K3, P1, K5, P1, C3F, P1, K4, P1, K3, P1, K6.
Round 22:	K2tog, P1, K3, P1, M1R, K5, P1, K3, P1, K4, P1, K3, P1, K6.
Round 23:	K1, P1, K3, P1, K6, M1L, P1, K3, P1, SSK, K2, P1, K3, P1, K6.
Round 24:	K1, P1, C3B, P1, K7, (P1, K3) twice, P1, C3F, P1, K6.
Round 25:	K1, P1, K3, P1, K7, P1, C3F, (P1, K3) twice, P1, K6.
Round 26:	K1, P1, K3, P1, K7, (P1, K3) twice, M1L, P1, K3, P1, SSK, K4.
Round 27:	K1, P1, K3, P1, K7, M1L, P1, K3, P1, SSK, K2, P1, K3, P1, K5.
Round 28:	K1, P1, C3F, P1, K8, (P1, K3) twice, P1, C3F, P1, K5.
Round 29:	K1, P1, K3, P1, K8, P1, C3F, (P1, K3) twice, P1, K5.
Round 30:	K1, M1L, P1, K3, P1, SSK, K6, (P1, K3) twice, M1L, P1, K3, P1, SSK, K3.
Round 31:	K2, P1, K3, P1, K7, M1L, P1, K3, P1, SSK, K2, P1, K3, P1, K4.
Round 32:	K2, P1, C3F, P1, K8, (P1, K3) twice, P1, C3F, P1, K4.
Round 33:	K2, P1, K3, P1, K8, P1, C3F, (P1, K3) twice, P1, K4.
Round 34:	K2, M1L, P1, K3, P1, SSK, K6, (P1, K3) twice, M1L, P1, K3, P1, SSK, K2.
Round 35:	(K3, P1) twice, K7, P1, K3, P1, K4, (P1, K3) twice.
Round 36:	K3, P1, C3F, P1, K7, P1, K3, P1, K4, P1, C3F, P1, K3.
Round 37:	(K3, P1) twice, K7, P1, C3B, P1, K4, (P1, K3) twice.
Round 38:	K3, M1L, P1, K3, P1, SSK, K5, P1, K3, P1, K4, M1L, P1, K3, P1, SSK, K1.
Round 39:	K4, P1, K3, P1, K4, SSK, P1, K3, P1, M1R, K5, P1, K3, P1, K2.
Round 40:	K4, P1, C3F, P1, K5, P1, K3, P1, K6, P1, C3F, P1, K2.

68 stitches (34 stitches twice)

Round 1:	K4, P1, K3, P1, K6, P1, C3B, P1, K7, P1, K3, P1, K2. (34 sts)
Round 2:	K4, M1L, P1, K3, P1, SSK, K4, P1, K3, P1, K7, P1, K3, P1, K2.
Round 3:	K5, (P1, K3) twice, K2tog, P1, K3, P1, M1R, K7, P1, K3, P1, K2.
Round 4:	K5, P1, C3F, P1, K4, P1, K3, P1, K8, P1, C3B, P1, K2.
Round 5:	K5, P1, K3, P1, K4, P1, C3B, P1, K8, P1, K3, P1, K2.
Round 6:	K5, P1, K3, P1, K4, P1, K3, P1, K6, K2tog, P1, K3, P1, M1R, K2.
Round 7:	K5, P1, K3, P1, K2, K2tog, P1, K3, P1, K8, (P1, K3) twice.
Round 8:	K5, P1, C3B, (P1, K3) twice, P1, K8, P1, C3B, P1, K3.
Round 9:	K5, (P1, K3) twice, P1, C3B, P1, K8, (P1, K3) twice.
Round 10:	K3, K2tog, P1, K3, P1, M1R, (K3, P1) twice, K6, K2tog, P1, K3, P1, M1R, K3.
Round 11:	K4, P1, K3, P1, K2, K2tog, P1, K3, P1, M1R, K7, P1, K3, P1, K4.
Round 12:	K4, P1, C3B, (P1, K3) twice, P1, K8, P1, C3B, P1, K4.
Round 13:	K4, (P1, K3) twice, P1, C3B, P1, K8, P1, K3, P1, K4.
Round 14:	K2, K2tog, P1, K3, P1, M1R, (K3, P1) twice, K6, K2tog, P1, K3, P1, M1R, K4.
Round 15:	(K3, P1) twice, K4, P1, K3, P1, K7, P1, K3, P1, K5.
Round 16:	K3, P1, C3B, P1, K4, P1, K3, P1, K7, P1, C3B, P1, K5.
Round 17:	(K3, P1) twice, K4, P1, C3F, P1, K7, P1, K3, P1, K5.
Round 18:	K1, K2tog, P1, K3, P1, M1R, K4, P1, K3, P1, K5, K2tog, P1, K3, P1, M1R, K5.
Round 19:	K2, P1, K3, P1, K5, M1L, K4, P1, SSK, K4, P1, K3, P1, K6.
Round 20:	K2, P1, C3B, P1, K6, P1, K3, P1, K5, P1, C3B, P1, K6.
Round 21:	K2, P1, K3, P1, K6, P1, C3F, P1, K5, P1, K3, P1, K6.
Round 22:	K2tog, P1, K3, P1, M1R, K6, P1, K3, P1, K5, P1, K3, P1, K6.
Round 23:	K1, P1, K3, P1, K7, M1L, P1, K3, P1, SSK, (K3, P1) twice, K6.
Round 24:	K1, P1, C3B, P1, K8, P1, K3, P1, K4, P1, C3F, P1, K6.
Round 25:	K1, P1, K3, P1, K8, P1, C3F, P1, K4, P1, K3, P1, K6.
Round 26:	K1, P1, K3, P1, K8, P1, K3, P1, K4, M1L, P1, K3, P1, SSK, K4.
Round 27:	K1, P1, K3, P1, K8, M1L, P1, K3, P1, SSK, (K3, P1) twice, K5.
Round 28:	K1, P1, C3F, P1, K9, P1, K3, P1, K4, P1, C3F, P1, K5.
Round 29:	K1, P1, K3, P1, K9, P1, C3F, P1, K4, P1, K3, P1, K5.
Round 30:	K1, M1L, P1, K3, P1, SSK, K7, P1, K3, P1, K4, M1L, P1, K3, P1, SSK, K3.
Round 31:	K2, P1, K3, P1, K8, M1L, P1, K3, P1, SSK, (K3, P1) twice, K4.
Round 32:	K2, P1, C3F, P1, K9, P1, K3, P1, K4, P1, C3F, P1, K4.
Round 33:	K2, P1, K3, P1, K9, P1, C3F, P1, K4, P1, K3, P1, K4.
Round 34:	K2, M1L, P1, K3, P1, SSK, K7, P1, K3, P1, K4, M1L, P1, K3, P1, SSK, K2.
Round 35:	(K3, P1) twice, K8, P1, K3, P1, K5, (P1, K3) twice.
Round 36:	K3, P1, C3F, P1, K8, P1, K3, P1, K5, P1, C3F, P1, K3.
Round 37:	(K3, P1) twice, K8, P1, C3B, P1, K5, (P1, K3) twice.
Round 38:	K3, M1L, P1, K3, P1, SSK, K6, P1, K3, P1, K5, M1L, P1, K3, P1, SSK, K1.
Round 39:	K4, P1, K3, P1, K5, SSK, P1, K3, P1, M1R, K6, P1, K3, P1, K2.
Round 40:	K4, P1, C3F, P1, K6, P1, K3, P1, K7, P1, C3F, P1, K2.

72 stitches (36 stitches twice)

Round 1:	K4, P1, K3, P1, K7, P1, C3B, P1, K8, P1, K3, P1, K2. (36 sts)
Round 2:	K4, M1L, P1, K3, P1, SSK, K5, P1, K3, P1, K8, P1, K3, P1, K2.
Round 3:	K5, P1, K3, P1, K4, K2tog, P1, K3, P1, M1R, K8, P1, K3, P1, K2.
Round 4:	K5, P1, C3F, P1, K5, P1, K3, P1, K9, P1, C3B, P1, K2.
Round 5:	K5, P1, K3, P1, K5, P1, C3B, P1, K9, P1, K3, P1, K2.
Round 6:	(K5, P1, K3, P1) twice, K7, K2tog, P1, K3, P1, M1R, K2.
Round 7:	K5, (P1, K3) twice, K2tog, P1, K3, P1, K9, (P1, K3) twice.
Round 8:	K5, P1, C3B, P1, K4, P1, K3, P1, K9, P1, C3B, P1, K3.
Round 9:	K5, P1, K3, P1, K4, P1, C3B, P1, K9, (P1, K3) twice.
Round 10:	K3, K2tog, P1, K3, P1, M1R, K4, P1, K3, P1, K7, K2tog, P1, K3, P1, M1R, K3.
Round 11:	K4, (P1, K3) twice, K2tog, P1, K3, P1, M1R, K8, P1, K3, P1, K4.
Round 12:	K4, P1, C3B, P1, K4, P1, K3, P1, K9, P1, C3B, P1, K4.
Round 13:	K4, P1, K3, P1, K4, P1, C3B, P1, K9, P1, K3, P1, K4.
Round 14:	K2, K2tog, P1, K3, P1, M1R, K4, P1, K3, P1, K7, K2tog, P1, K3, P1, M1R, K4.
Round 15:	(K3, P1) twice, K5, P1, K3, P1, K8, P1, K3, P1, K5.
Round 16:	K3, P1, C3B, P1, K5, P1, K3, P1, K8, P1, C3B, P1, K5.
Round 17:	(K3, P1) twice, K5, P1, C3F, P1, K8, P1, K3, P1, K5.
Round 18:	K1, K2tog, P1, K3, P1, M1R, K5, P1, K3, P1, K6, K2tog, P1, K3, P1, M1R, K5.
Round 19:	K2, P1, K3, P1, K6, M1L, K4, P1, SSK, K5, P1, K3, P1, K6.
Round 20:	K2, P1, C3B, P1, K7, P1, K3, P1, K6, P1, C3B, P1, K6.
Round 21:	K2, P1, K3, P1, K7, P1, C3F, P1, K6, P1, K3, P1, K6.
Round 22:	K2tog, P1, K3, P1, M1R, K7, (P1, K3, P1, K6) twice.
Round 23:	K1, P1, K3, P1, K8, M1L, P1, K3, P1, SSK, K4, P1, K3, P1, K6.
Round 24:	K1, P1, C3B, P1, K9, P1, K3, P1, K5, P1, C3F, P1, K6.
Round 25:	K1, P1, K3, P1, K9, P1, C3F, P1, K5, P1, K3, P1, K6.
Round 26:	K1, P1, K3, P1, K9, P1, K3, P1, K5, M1L, P1, K3, P1, SSK, K4.
Round 27:	K1, P1, K3, P1, K9, M1L, P1, K3, P1, SSK, K4, P1, K3, P1, K5.
Round 28:	K1, P1, C3F, P1, K10, P1, K3, P1, K5, P1, C3F, P1, K5.
Round 29:	K1, P1, K3, P1, K10, P1, C3F, P1, K5, P1, K3, P1, K5.
Round 30:	K1, M1L, P1, K3, P1, SSK, K8, P1, K3, P1, K5, M1L, P1, K3, P1, SSK, K3.
Round 31:	K2, P1, K3, P1, K9, M1L, P1, K3, P1, SSK, K4, P1, K3, P1, K4.
Round 32:	K2, P1, C3F, P1, K10, P1, K3, P1, K5, P1, C3F, P1, K4.
Round 33:	K2, P1, K3, P1, K10, P1, C3F, P1, K5, P1, K3, P1, K4.
Round 34:	K2, M1L, P1, K3, P1, SSK, K8, P1, K3, P1, K5, M1L, P1, K3, P1, SSK, K2.
Round 35:	(K3, P1) twice, K9, P1, K3, P1, K6, (P1, K3) twice.
Round 36:	K3, P1, C3F, P1, K9, P1, K3, P1, K6, P1, C3F, P1, K3.
Round 37:	(K3, P1) twice, K9, P1, C3B, P1, K6, (P1, K3) twice.
Round 38:	K3, M1L, P1, K3, P1, SSK, K7, P1, K3, P1, K6, M1L, P1, K3, P1, SSK, K1.
Round 39:	K4, P1, K3, P1, K6, SSK, P1, K3, P1, M1R, K7, P1, K3, P1, K2.
Round 40:	K4, P1, C3F, P1, K7, P1, K3, P1, K8, P1, C3F, P1, K2.

76 stitches (38 stitches twice)

Round 1:	K5, P1, K3, P1, K7, P1, C3B, P1, K8, (P1, K3) twice. (38 sts)
Round 2:	K5, M1L, P1, K3, P1, SSK, K5, P1, K3, P1, K8, (P1, K3) twice.
Round 3:	K6, P1, K3, P1, K4, K2tog, P1, K3, P1, M1R, K8, (P1, K3) twice.
Round 4:	K6, P1, C3F, P1, K5, P1, K3, P1, K9, P1, C3B, P1, K3.
Round 5:	K6, P1, K3, P1, K5, P1, C3B, P1, K9, (P1, K3) twice.
Round 6:	K6, P1, K3, P1, K5, P1, K3, P1, K7, K2tog, P1, K3, P1, M1R, K3.
Round 7:	K6, (P1, K3) twice, K2tog, P1, K3, P1, K9, P1, K3, P1, K4.
Round 8:	K6, P1, C3B, P1, K4, P1, K3, P1, K9, P1, C3B, P1, K4.
Round 9:	K6, P1, K3, P1, K4, P1, C3B, P1, K9, P1, K3, P1, K4.
Round 10:	K4, K2tog, P1, K3, P1, M1R, K4, P1, K3, P1, K7, K2tog, P1, K3, P1, M1R, K4.
Round 11:	K5, (P1, K3) twice, K2tog, P1, K3, P1, M1R, K8, P1, K3, P1, K5.
Round 12:	K5, P1, C3B, P1, K4, P1, K3, P1, K9, P1, C3B, P1, K5.
Round 13:	K5, P1, K3, P1, K4, P1, C3B, P1, K9, P1, K3, P1, K5.
Round 14:	K3, K2tog, P1, K3, P1, M1R, K4, P1, K3, P1, K7, K2tog, P1, K3, P1, M1R, K5.
Round 15:	K4, P1, K3, P1, K5, P1, K3, P1, K8, P1, K3, P1, K6.
Round 16:	K4, P1, C3B, P1, K5, P1, K3, P1, K8, P1, C3B, P1, K6.
Round 17:	K4, P1, K3, P1, K5, P1, C3F, P1, K8, P1, K3, P1, K6.
Round 18:	K2, K2tog, P1, K3, P1, M1R, K5, P1, K3, P1, K6, K2tog, P1, K3, P1, M1R, K6.
Round 19:	(K3, P1) twice, K6, M1L, K4, P1, SSK, K5, P1, K3, P1, K7.
Round 20:	K3, P1, C3B, P1, K7, P1, K3, P1, K6, P1, C3B, P1, K7.
Round 21:	(K3, P1) twice, K7, P1, C3F, P1, K6, P1, K3, P1, K7.
Round 22:	K1, K2tog, P1, K3, P1, M1R, K7, P1, K3, P1, K6, P1, K3, P1, K7.
Round 23:	K2, P1, K3, P1, K8, M1L, P1, K3, P1, SSK, K4, P1, K3, P1, K7.
Round 24:	K2, P1, C3B, P1, K9, P1, K3, P1, K5, P1, C3F, P1, K7.
Round 25:	K2, P1, K3, P1, K9, P1, C3F, P1, K5, P1, K3, P1, K7.
Round 26:	K2, P1, K3, P1, K9, P1, K3, P1, K5, M1L, P1, K3, P1, SSK, K5.
Round 27:	K2, P1, K3, P1, K9, M1L, P1, K3, P1, SSK, K4, P1, K3, P1, K6.
Round 28:	K2, P1, C3F, P1, K10, P1, K3, P1, K5, P1, C3F, P1, K6.
Round 29:	K2, P1, K3, P1, K10, P1, C3F, P1, K5, P1, K3, P1, K6.
Round 30:	K2, M1L, P1, K3, P1, SSK, K8, P1, K3, P1, K5, M1L, P1, K3, P1, SSK, K4.
Round 31:	(K3, P1) twice, K9, M1L, P1, K3, P1, SSK, K4, P1, K3, P1, K5.
Round 32:	K3, P1, C3F, P1, K10, P1, K3, P1, K5, P1, C3F, P1, K5.
Round 33:	(K3, P1) twice, K10, P1, C3F, P1, K5, P1, K3, P1, K5.
Round 34:	K3, M1L, P1, K3, P1, SSK, K8, P1, K3, P1, K5, M1L, P1, K3, P1, SSK, K3.
Round 35:	K4, P1, K3, P1, K9, P1, K3, P1, K6, P1, K3, P1, K4.
Round 36:	K4, P1, C3F, P1, K9, P1, K3, P1, K6, P1, C3F, P1, K4.
Round 37:	K4, P1, K3, P1, K9, P1, C3B, P1, K6, P1, K3, P1, K4.
Round 38:	K4, M1L, P1, K3, P1, SSK, K7, P1, K3, P1, K6, M1L, P1, K3, P1, SSK, K2.
Round 39:	K5, P1, K3, P1, K6, SSK, P1, K3, P1, M1R, K7, (P1, K3) twice.
Round 40:	K5, P1, C3F, P1, K7, P1, K3, P1, K8, P1, C3F, P1, K3.

Right foot

Cast on 64 [68:72:76] stitches using 3.0 mm double pointed needles. Remember that you will need to work the chart stitches twice. **The pattern has been written for a cast on with straight needles – if you want to join straight into the round, work round 1 twice and omit round 2 of the cuff pattern.**

Row 1:   Work round 1 of cuff using chart (reading right to left) or written instructions, turn.
Row 2:   Work round 2 of cuff using chart (reading left to right) or written instructions, turn.

Change to a 2.5 mm short circular needle, magic loop or divide the stitches across DPNs and join into a circle, place marker. You might find it helps to place a second marker to indicate where the chart repeats. You will sew up the small gap where you knitted the first two rows later.

Continue to work cuff using chart for right foot (reading from right to left) or written instructions for 14 more rounds.

64 stitches (32 stitches twice)

Round 1:   (K2, P1, K3, P1, K2, P2) twice, K1, P1, K3, P1, K2, P2.
Round 2:   P2, K1, P3, (K1, P2, K2, P2) twice, K2, P1, K1, P3, K1, P2, K2.
Round 3:   K2, P1, C3F, P1, K2, P2, K2, P1, K3, P1, K2, P2, K1, P1, C3F, P1, K2, P2.
Round 4:   K2, P1, K3, P1, K2, P2, K2, P1, C3F, P1, K2, P2, K1, P1, K3, P1, K2, P2.
Round 5:   Repeat round 1.
Round 6:   Repeat round 1.
Round 7:   Repeat round 3.
Round 8:   Repeat round 1.
Round 9:   Repeat round 4.
Rounds 10 - 13: Repeat rounds 6 - 9.
Round 14:   Repeat round 1.
Round 15:   Repeat round 3.
Round 16:   Repeat round 1.

68 stitches (34 stitches twice)

Round 1:   K2, P1, K3, P1, K2, p2, (K3, P1) twice, K2, p2, K2, P1, K3, P1, K2, p2. (34 sts)
Round 2:   P2, K1, p3, K1, (p2, K2) twice, p3, K1, p2, K2, p2, K1, p3, K1, p2, K2.
Round 3:   K2, P1, C3F, P1, (K2, p2) twice, K3, P1, K2, p2, K2, P1, C3F, P1, K2, p2.
Round 4:   K2, P1, K3, P1, (K2, p2) twice, C3B, P1, K2, p2, K2, P1, K3, P1, K2, p2.
Round 5:   K2, P1, K3, P1, (K2, p2) twice, K3, P1, K2, p2, K2, P1, K3, P1, K2, p2.
Round 6:   Repeat round 5.
Round 7:   Repeat round 3.
Round 8:   Repeat round 5.
Round 9:   Repeat round 4.
Rounds 10-13:   Repeat rounds 6 - 9.
Round 14:   Repeat round 5.

| Round 15: | Repeat round 3. |
| Round 16: | Repeat round 5. |

72 stitches (36 stitches twice)

Round 1:	K2, P1, K3, P1, K2, P2, K4, P1, K3, P1, K2, P2, (K3, P1) twice, K2, P2. (36 sts)
Round 2:	P2, K1, P3, K2, ((P2, K2) twice, P3, K1) twice, P2, K2.
Round 3:	K2, P1, C3F, (P2, K2) twice, P2, K3, P1, (K2, P2) twice, C3F, P1, K2, P2.
Round 4:	K2, P1, K3, (P2, K2) twice, P2, C3B, P1, (K2, P2) twice, K3, P1, K2, P2.
Round 5:	K2, P1, K3, P2, ((K2, P2) twice, K3, P1) twice, K2, P2.
Round 6:	Repeat round 5.
Round 7:	Repeat round 3.
Round 8:	Repeat round 5.
Round 9:	Repeat round 4.
Rounds 10-13:	Repeat rounds 6-9.
Round 14:	Repeat round 5.
Round 15:	Repeat round 3.
Round 16:	Repeat round 5.

76 stitches (38 sts twice)

Round 1:	P2, K1, P1, K3, P1, K1, p2, K2, p2, K1, P1, K3, P1, K1, p5, K1, P1, K3, P1, K1, P2, K2. (38 sts)
Round 2:	K2, P1, K1, P3, K2, P1, K1, P2, K4, P3, K1, (P1, K2) twice, P1, K1, P3, (K1, P2) twice.
Round 3:	P2, K1, P1, C3F, (P2, K1) 3 times, P1, K3, P1, (K1, P2) twice, K1, P1, C3F, P1, K1, P2, K2.
Round 4:	P2, K1, P1, K3, (P2, K1) 3 times, P1, C3B, P1, (K1, P2) twice, K1, P1, K3, P1, K1, P2, K2.
Round 5:	P2, K1, P1, K3, P2, ((K1, P2) twice, K1, P1, K3, P1) twice, K1, P2, K2.
Round 6:	Repeat round 5.
Round 7:	Repeat round 3.
Round 8:	Repeat round 5.
Round 9:	Repeat round 4.
Rounds 10-13:	Repeat rounds 6-9.
Round 14:	Repeat round 5.
Round 15:	Repeat round 3.
Round 16:	Repeat round 5.

Right Leg

Using either the charts or the written pattern for right leg, continue to knit each round until leg measures 6 [7] inches; 15 [17] cm or desired length from cast on edge, remembering which round of the pattern you finished on for the heel flap as you will need this later.

64 stitches (32 stitches twice)

Round 1:	K2, P1, K3, P1, K6, P1, C3F, P1, K5, P1, K3, P1, K4. (32 sts)
Round 2:	K2, P1, K3, P1, K6, (P1, K3) twice, K2tog, P1, K3, P1, M1R, K4.
Round 3:	K2, P1, K3, P1, K6, M1L, P1, K3, P1, SSK, K2, P1, K3, P1, K5.
Round 4:	K2, P1, C3F, P1, K7, (P1, K3) twice, P1, C3B, P1, K5.
Round 5:	K2, P1, K3, P1, K7, P1, C3F, (P1, K3) twice, P1, K5.
Round 6:	K2, M1L, P1, K3, P1, SSK, K5, (P1, K3) 3 times, P1, K5.
Round 7:	(K3, P1) twice, K7, P1, K3, P1, SSK, K1, P1, K3, P1, K5.
Round 8:	K3, P1, C3F, P1, K7, P1, K3, P1, K2, P1, C3F, P1, K5.
Round 9:	(K3, P1) twice, K7, P1, C3F, P1, K2, P1, K3, P1, K5.
Round 10:	K3, M1L, P1, K3, P1, SSK, K5, P1, K3, P1, K2, M1L, P1, K3, P1, SSK, K3.
Round 11:	K4, P1, K3, P1, K6, M1L, P1, K3, P1, SSK, K1, P1, K3, P1, K4.
Round 12:	K4, P1, C3F, P1, K7, P1, K3, P1, K2, P1, C3F, P1, K4.
Round 13:	K4, P1, K3, P1, K7, P1, C3F, P1, K2, P1, K3, P1, K4.
Round 14:	K4, M1L, P1, K3, P1, SSK, K5, P1, K3, P1, K2, M1L, P1, K3, P1, SSK, K2.
Round 15:	K5, P1, K3, P1, K6, (P1, K3) 4 times.
Round 16:	K5, P1, C3F, P1, K6, (P1, K3) twice, P1, C3F, P1, K3.
Round 17:	K5, P1, K3, P1, K6, P1, C3B, (P1, K3) 3 times.
Round 18:	K5, M1L, P1, K3, P1, SSK, K4, (P1, K3) twice, M1L, P1, K3, P1, SSK, K1.
Round 19:	K6, (P1, K3) twice, K2tog, P1, K4, M1R, K4, P1, K3, P1, K2.
Round 20:	K6, P1, C3F, P1, K4, P1, K3, P1, K5, P1, C3F, P1, K2.
Round 21:	K6, P1, K3, P1, K4, P1, C3B, P1, K5, P1, K3, P1, K2.
Round 22:	K6, P1, K3, P1, K4, P1, K3, P1, K5, M1L, P1, K3, P1, SSK.
Round 23:	K6, P1, K3, P1, K2, K2tog, P1, K3, P1, M1R, K6, P1, K3, P1, K1.
Round 24:	K6, P1, C3B, (P1, K3) twice, P1, K7, P1, C3F, P1, K1.
Round 25:	K6, (P1, K3) twice, P1, C3B, P1, K7, P1, K3, P1, K1.
Round 26:	K4, K2tog, P1, K3, P1, M1R, (K3, P1) twice, K7, P1, K3, P1, K1.
Round 27:	K5, P1, K3, P1, K2, K2tog, P1, K3, P1, M1R, K7, P1, K3, P1, K1.
Round 28:	K5, P1, C3B, (P1, K3) twice, P1, K8, P1, C3B, P1, K1.
Round 29:	K5, (P1, K3) twice, P1, C3B, P1, K8, P1, K3, P1, K1.
Round 30:	K3, K2tog, P1, K3, P1, M1R, (K3, P1) twice, K6, K2tog, P1, K3, P1, M1R, K1.
Round 31:	K4, P1, K3, P1, K2, K2tog, P1, K3, P1, M1R, K7, P1, K3, P1, K2.
Round 32:	K4, P1, C3B, (P1, K3) twice, P1, K8, P1, C3B, P1, K2.
Round 33:	K4, (P1, K3) twice, P1, C3B, P1, K8, P1, K3, P1, K2.
Round 34:	K2, K2tog, P1, K3, P1, M1R, (K3, P1) twice, K6, K2tog, P1, K3, P1, M1R, K2.
Round 35:	(K3, P1) twice, K4, P1, K3, P1, K7, (P1, K3) twice.
Round 36:	K3, P1, C3B, P1, K4, P1, K3, P1, K7, P1, C3B, P1, K3.
Round 37:	(K3, P1) twice, K4, P1, C3F, P1, K7, (P1, K3) twice.
Round 38:	K1, K2tog, P1, K3, P1, M1R, K4, P1, K3, P1, K5, K2tog, P1, K3, P1, M1R, K3.
Round 39:	K2, P1, K3, P1, K5, M1L, P1, K3, P1, K2tog, K4, P1, K3, P1, K4.
Round 40:	K2, P1, C3B, P1, K6, P1, K3, P1, K5, P1, C3B, P1, K4.

68 stitches (34 stitches twice)

Round 1:	K2, P1, K3, P1, K7, P1, C3F, P1, K6, P1, K3, P1, K4. (34 sts)
Round 2:	K2, P1, K3, P1, K7, P1, K3, P1, K4, K2tog, P1, K3, P1, M1R, K4.
Round 3:	K2, P1, K3, P1, K7, M1L, P1, K3, P1, SSK, (K3, P1) twice, K5.
Round 4:	K2, P1, C3F, P1, K8, P1, K3, P1, K4, P1, C3B, P1, K5.
Round 5:	K2, P1, K3, P1, K8, P1, C3F, P1, K4, P1, K3, P1, K5.
Round 6:	K2, M1L, P1, K3, P1, SSK, K6, P1, K3, P1, K4, P1, K3, P1, K5.
Round 7:	(K3, P1) twice, K8, P1, K3, P1, SSK, K2, P1, K3, P1, K5.
Round 8:	K3, P1, C3F, P1, K8, (P1, K3) twice, P1, C3F, P1, K5.
Round 9:	(K3, P1) twice, K8, P1, C3F, (P1, K3) twice, P1, K5.
Round 10:	K3, M1L, P1, K3, P1, SSK, K6, (P1, K3) twice, M1L, P1, K3, P1, SSK, K3.
Round 11:	K4, P1, K3, P1, K7, M1L, P1, K3, P1, SSK, K2, P1, K3, P1, K4.
Round 12:	K4, P1, C3F, P1, K8, (P1, K3) twice, P1, C3F, P1, K4.
Round 13:	K4, P1, K3, P1, K8, P1, C3F, (P1, K3) twice, P1, K4.
Round 14:	K4, M1L, P1, K3, P1, SSK, K6, (P1, K3) twice, M1L, P1, K3, P1, SSK, K2.
Round 15:	K5, P1, K3, P1, K7, P1, K3, P1, K4, (P1, K3) twice.
Round 16:	K5, P1, C3F, P1, K7, P1, K3, P1, K4, P1, C3F, P1, K3.
Round 17:	K5, P1, K3, P1, K7, P1, C3B, P1, K4, (P1, K3) twice.
Round 18:	K5, M1L, P1, K3, P1, SSK, K5, P1, K3, P1, K4, M1L, P1, K3, P1, SSK, K1.
Round 19:	K6, P1, K3, P1, K4, K2tog, P1, K4, M1R, K5, P1, K3, P1, K2.
Round 20:	K6, P1, C3F, P1, K5, P1, K3, P1, K6, P1, C3F, P1, K2.
Round 21:	K6, P1, K3, P1, K5, P1, C3B, P1, K6, P1, K3, P1, K2.
Round 22:	K6, P1, K3, P1, K5, P1, K3, P1, K6, M1L, P1, K3, P1, SSK.
Round 23:	K6, (P1, K3) twice, K2tog, P1, K3, P1, M1R, K7, P1, K3, P1, K1.
Round 24:	K6, P1, C3B, P1, K4, P1, K3, P1, K8, P1, C3F, P1, K1.
Round 25:	K6, P1, K3, P1, K4, P1, C3B, P1, K8, P1, K3, P1, K1.
Round 26:	K4, K2tog, P1, K3, P1, M1R, K4, P1, K3, P1, K8, P1, K3, P1, K1.
Round 27:	K5, (P1, K3) twice, K2tog, P1, K3, P1, M1R, K8, P1, K3, P1, K1.
Round 28:	K5, P1, C3B, P1, K4, P1, K3, P1, K9, P1, C3B, P1, K1.
Round 29:	K5, P1, K3, P1, K4, P1, C3B, P1, K9, P1, K3, P1, K1.
Round 30:	K3, K2tog, P1, K3, P1, M1R, K4, P1, K3, P1, K7, K2tog, P1, K3, P1, M1R, K1.
Round 31:	K4, (P1, K3) twice, K2tog, P1, K3, P1, M1R, K8, P1, K3, P1, K2.
Round 32:	K4, P1, C3B, P1, K4, P1, K3, P1, K9, P1, C3B, P1, K2.
Round 33:	K4, P1, K3, P1, K4, P1, C3B, P1, K9, P1, K3, P1, K2.
Round 34:	K2, K2tog, P1, K3, P1, M1R, K4, P1, K3, P1, K7, K2tog, P1, K3, P1, M1R, K2.
Round 35:	(K3, P1) twice, K5, P1, K3, P1, K8, (P1, K3) twice.
Round 36:	K3, P1, C3B, P1, K5, P1, K3, P1, K8, P1, C3B, P1, K3.
Round 37:	(K3, P1) twice, K5, P1, C3F, P1, K8, (P1, K3) twice.
Round 38:	K1, K2tog, P1, K3, P1, M1R, K5, P1, K3, P1, K6, K2tog, P1, K3, P1, M1R, K3.
Round 39:	K2, P1, K3, P1, K6, M1L, P1, K3, P1, K2tog, K5, P1, K3, P1, K4.
Round 40:	K2, P1, C3B, P1, K7, P1, K3, P1, K6, P1, C3B, P1, K4.

72 stitches (36 stitches twice)

Round 1:	K2, P1, K3, P1, K8, P1, C3F, P1, K7, P1, K3, P1, K4. (36 sts)
Round 2:	K2, P1, K3, P1, K8, P1, K3, P1, K5, K2tog, P1, K3, P1, M1R, K4.
Round 3:	K2, P1, K3, P1, K8, M1L, P1, K3, P1, SSK, K4, P1, K3, P1, K5.
Round 4:	K2, P1, C3F, P1, K9, P1, K3, P1, K5, P1, C3B, P1, K5.
Round 5:	K2, P1, K3, P1, K9, P1, C3F, P1, K5, P1, K3, P1, K5.
Round 6:	K2, M1L, P1, K3, P1, SSK, K7, (P1, K3, P1, K5) twice.
Round 7:	(K3, P1) twice, K9, P1, K3, P1, SSK, (K3, P1) twice, K5.
Round 8:	K3, P1, C3F, P1, K9, P1, K3, P1, K4, P1, C3F, P1, K5.
Round 9:	(K3, P1) twice, K9, P1, C3F, P1, K4, P1, K3, P1, K5.
Round 10:	K3, M1L, P1, K3, P1, SSK, K7, P1, K3, P1, K4, M1L, P1, K3, P1, SSK, K3.
Round 11:	K4, P1, K3, P1, K8, M1L, P1, K3, P1, SSK, (K3, P1) twice, K4.
Round 12:	K4, P1, C3F, P1, K9, P1, K3, P1, K4, P1, C3F, P1, K4.
Round 13:	K4, P1, K3, P1, K9, P1, C3F, P1, K4, P1, K3, P1, K4.
Round 14:	K4, M1L, P1, K3, P1, SSK, K7, P1, K3, P1, K4, M1L, P1, K3, P1, SSK, K2.
Round 15:	K5, P1, K3, P1, K8, P1, K3, P1, K5, (P1, K3) twice.
Round 16:	K5, P1, C3F, P1, K8, P1, K3, P1, K5, P1, C3F, P1, K3.
Round 17:	K5, P1, K3, P1, K8, P1, C3B, P1, K5, (P1, K3) twice.
Round 18:	K5, M1L, P1, K3, P1, SSK, K6, P1, K3, P1, K5, M1L, P1, K3, P1, SSK, K1.
Round 19:	K6, P1, K3, P1, K5, K2tog, P1, K4, M1R, K6, P1, K3, P1, K2.
Round 20:	K6, P1, C3F, P1, K6, P1, K3, P1, K7, P1, C3F, P1, K2.
Round 21:	K6, P1, K3, P1, K6, P1, C3B, P1, K7, P1, K3, P1, K2.
Round 22:	(K6, P1, K3, P1) twice, K7, M1L, P1, K3, P1, SSK.
Round 23:	K6, P1, K3, P1, K4, K2tog, P1, K3, P1, M1R, K8, P1, K3, P1, K1.
Round 24:	K6, P1, C3B, P1, K5, P1, K3, P1, K9, P1, C3F, P1, K1.
Round 25:	K6, P1, K3, P1, K5, P1, C3B, P1, K9, P1, K3, P1, K1.
Round 26:	K4, K2tog, P1, K3, P1, M1R, K5, P1, K3, P1, K9, P1, K3, P1, K1.
Round 27:	K5, P1, K3, P1, K4, K2tog, P1, K3, P1, M1R, K9, P1, K3, P1, K1.
Round 28:	K5, P1, C3B, P1, K5, P1, K3, P1, K10, P1, C3B, P1, K1.
Round 29:	K5, P1, K3, P1, K5, P1, C3B, P1, K10, P1, K3, P1, K1.
Round 30:	K3, K2tog, P1, K3, P1, M1R, K5, P1, K3, P1, K8, K2tog, P1, K3, P1, M1R, K1.
Round 31:	K4, P1, K3, P1, K4, K2tog, P1, K3, P1, M1R, K9, P1, K3, P1, K2.
Round 32:	K4, P1, C3B, P1, K5, P1, K3, P1, K10, P1, C3B, P1, K2.
Round 33:	K4, P1, K3, P1, K5, P1, C3B, P1, K10, P1, K3, P1, K2.
Round 34:	K2, K2tog, P1, K3, P1, M1R, K5, P1, K3, P1, K8, K2tog, P1, K3, P1, M1R, K2.
Round 35:	(K3, P1) twice, K6, P1, K3, P1, K9, (P1, K3) twice.
Round 36:	K3, P1, C3B, P1, K6, P1, K3, P1, K9, P1, C3B, P1, K3.
Round 37:	(K3, P1) twice, K6, P1, C3F, P1, K9, (P1, K3) twice.
Round 38:	K1, K2tog, P1, K3, P1, M1R, K6, P1, K3, P1, K7, K2tog, P1, K3, P1, M1R, K3.
Round 39:	K2, P1, K3, P1, K7, M1L, P1, K3, P1, K2tog, K6, P1, K3, P1, K4.
Round 40:	K2, P1, C3B, P1, K8, P1, K3, P1, K7, P1, C3B, P1, K4.

76 stitches (38 stitches twice)

Round 1:	(K3, P1) twice, K8, P1, C3F, P1, K7, P1, K3, P1, K5. (38 sts)
Round 2:	(K3, P1) twice, K8, P1, K3, P1, K5, K2tog, P1, K3, P1, M1R, K5.
Round 3:	(K3, P1) twice, K8, M1L, P1, K3, P1, SSK, K4, P1, K3, P1, K6.
Round 4:	K3, P1, C3F, P1, K9, P1, K3, P1, K5, P1, C3B, P1, K6.
Round 5:	(K3, P1) twice, K9, P1, C3F, P1, K5, P1, K3, P1, K6.
Round 6:	K3, M1L, P1, K3, P1, SSK, K7, P1, K3, P1, K5, P1, K3, P1, K6.
Round 7:	K4, P1, K3, P1, K9, P1, K3, P1, SSK, (K3, P1) twice, K6.
Round 8:	K4, P1, C3F, P1, K9, P1, K3, P1, K4, P1, C3F, P1, K6.
Round 9:	K4, P1, K3, P1, K9, P1, C3F, P1, K4, P1, K3, P1, K6.
Round 10:	K4, M1L, P1, K3, P1, SSK, K7, P1, K3, P1, K4, M1L, P1, K3, P1, SSK, K4.
Round 11:	K5, P1, K3, P1, K8, M1L, P1, K3, P1, SSK, (K3, P1) twice, K5.
Round 12:	K5, P1, C3F, P1, K9, P1, K3, P1, K4, P1, C3F, P1, K5.
Round 13:	K5, P1, K3, P1, K9, P1, C3F, P1, K4, P1, K3, P1, K5.
Round 14:	K5, M1L, P1, K3, P1, SSK, K7, P1, K3, P1, K4, M1L, P1, K3, P1, SSK, K3.
Round 15:	K6, P1, K3, P1, K8, P1, K3, P1, K5, P1, K3, P1, K4.
Round 16:	K6, P1, C3F, P1, K8, P1, K3, P1, K5, P1, C3F, P1, K4.
Round 17:	K6, P1, K3, P1, K8, P1, C3B, P1, K5, P1, K3, P1, K4.
Round 18:	K6, M1L, P1, K3, P1, SSK, K6, P1, K3, P1, K5, M1L, P1, K3, P1, SSK, K2.
Round 19:	K7, P1, K3, P1, K5, K2tog, P1, K4, M1R, K6, (P1, K3) twice.
Round 20:	K7, P1, C3F, P1, K6, P1, K3, P1, K7, P1, C3F, P1, K3.
Round 21:	K7, P1, K3, P1, K6, P1, C3B, P1, K7, (P1, K3) twice.
Round 22:	K7, P1, K3, P1, K6, P1, K3, P1, K7, M1L, P1, K3, P1, SSK, K1.
Round 23:	K7, P1, K3, P1, K4, K2tog, P1, K3, P1, M1R, K8, P1, K3, P1, K2.
Round 24:	K7, P1, C3B, P1, K5, P1, K3, P1, K9, P1, C3F, P1, K2.
Round 25:	K7, P1, K3, P1, K5, P1, C3B, P1, K9, P1, K3, P1, K2.
Round 26:	K5, K2tog, P1, K3, P1, M1R, K5, P1, K3, P1, K9, P1, K3, P1, K2.
Round 27:	K6, P1, K3, P1, K4, K2tog, P1, K3, P1, M1R, K9, P1, K3, P1, K2.
Round 28:	K6, P1, C3B, P1, K5, P1, K3, P1, K10, P1, C3B, P1, K2.
Round 29:	K6, P1, K3, P1, K5, P1, C3B, P1, K10, P1, K3, P1, K2.
Round 30:	K4, K2tog, P1, K3, P1, M1R, K5, P1, K3, P1, K8, K2tog, P1, K3, P1, M1R, K2.
Round 31:	K5, P1, K3, P1, K4, K2tog, P1, K3, P1, M1R, K9, (P1, K3) twice.
Round 32:	K5, P1, C3B, P1, K5, P1, K3, P1, K10, P1, C3B, P1, K3.
Round 33:	K5, P1, K3, P1, K5, P1, C3B, P1, K10, (P1, K3) twice.
Round 34:	K3, K2tog, P1, K3, P1, M1R, K5, P1, K3, P1, K8, K2tog, P1, K3, P1, M1R, K3.
Round 35:	K4, P1, K3, P1, K6, P1, K3, P1, K9, P1, K3, P1, K4.
Round 36:	K4, P1, C3B, P1, K6, P1, K3, P1, K9, P1, C3B, P1, K4.
Round 37:	K4, P1, K3, P1, K6, P1, C3F, P1, K9, P1, K3, P1, K4.
Round 38:	K2, K2tog, P1, K3, P1, M1R, K6, P1, K3, P1, K7, K2tog, P1, K3, P1, M1R, K4.
Round 39:	(K3, P1) twice, K7, M1L, P1, K3, P1, K2tog, K6, P1, K3, P1, K5.
Round 40:	K3, P1, C3B, P1, K8, P1, K3, P1, K7, P1, C3B, P1, K5.

Heel Flap – make both the same

Change to 2.5 mm DPNs if you are using a short circular needle. There is no need to use DPNs if you are using magic loop. You may prefer to place the spare stitches from the top of the foot onto a stitch holder if you are using a short circular or DPNs whilst you work the heel.

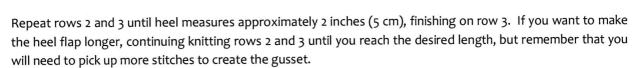

Row 1:   K2, (Slip 1, K1) until you have 32 [34:36:38] stitches on your needle, turn.
Row 2:   Slip 1, P to end, turn.
Row 3:   (Slip 1, K1) to end, turn.

Repeat rows 2 and 3 until heel measures approximately 2 inches (5 cm), finishing on row 3. If you want to make the heel flap longer, continuing knitting rows 2 and 3 until you reach the desired length, but remember that you will need to pick up more stitches to create the gusset.

Turn heel

Row 1:   Slip1, P17 [P18:P19:P20], P2tog, P1, turn.
Row 2:   Slip 1, K5, SSK, K1, turn.
Row 3:   Slip 1, P6, P2tog, P1, turn.
Row 4:   Slip 1, K7, SSK, K1, turn.

Continue in this way, adding one stitch between slip stitch and SSK or P2tog on each row (ie, Row 5: Slip 1, **P8**, P2tog, P1; Row 6: Slip 1, **K9**, SSK, K1, etc) until all of the heel stitches are used.

Knit across the heel stitches if required to bring you to the left hand side of the heel flap (with the outside of the flap facing you) ready to pick up 1 stitch for every 2 rows knitted. Remember that if you made the heel flap bigger, you will need to pick up more stitches. Once you have picked up the stitches, place marker. Knit across the top of the foot stitches in pattern (start on the pattern row after the one where you finished for the heel flap), place marker, then pick up 1 stitch for every 2 rows of heel flap knitted up the other side of the heel.

Note: If you are using DPNs and/or have placed your stitches on a stitch holder, you can arrange the needles as follows: Needle 1 for stitches across heel, Needle 2 for picked-up stitches down side of foot, Needle 3 for stitches across top of foot (knit stitches off stitch holder if required), Needle 4 for picked-up stitches on other side of foot. You may find that stitch markers are not required at first.

Shape gusset

Continue to use the pattern from the leg chart for whichever foot you are working. You will only work the chart stitches once for the foot.

Round 1:   K to 3 sts before the marker, K2tog, K1, slip marker, knit in pattern to next marker, slip marker, K1, SSK, K to marker.
Round 2:   Slip marker, knit in pattern to next marker, slip marker, knit to 3 sts before marker.

Round 3:   K2tog, K1, slip marker, knit in pattern to next marker, slip marker, K1, SSK, K to marker.

Repeat rounds 2 and 3 to shape the gusset. Continue in this way, decreasing by two stitches at the gusset on every other round until there are 64 [68:72:76] stitches on the needle.

Once you have reached the required number of stitches, continue to knit each round in pattern until you reach approximately 2 inches (5 cm) before the desired length ready to start the toes. Don't be afraid to try your sock on before decreasing for the toes!

Toes

Note: At some point whilst decreasing for the toes, if you are using a short circular needle you may need to change back to DPNs or use the magic loop method as the number of stitches becomes too small for the circular. It's up to you when you choose to do that, and how you distribute the stitches across the needles; just keep following the pattern as set.

You may choose to work a plain toe, but if you prefer to continue the pattern down across the toes, you will need to take the decreases into account. Whenever there is an increase stitch, there is a corresponding decrease stitch and you need both of those to keep the stitch count correct across the toes; if your decreases mean that you can only work one, then miss it out – it's better to work on the right number of stitches and the missing decrease won't be noticed on the toes.

Round 1:   K1, SSK, K26 [28:30:32] sts in pattern if desired, K2tog, K1, place marker, K1, SSK, K26 [28:30:32] sts, K2tog, K1. (60 [64:68:72] sts)
Round 2:   K3, work across top of foot in pattern if desired, K3, slip marker, K to end of round, slip marker
Round 3:   K1, SSK, K in pattern to 3 sts before marker, K2tog, K1, slip marker, K1, SSK, K to 3 sts before marker, K2tog, K1. (56 [60:64:68] sts)

Repeat rounds 2 and 3 until you have 28 stitches left and divide these between two needles so that front and back of socks match.

Graft the toes using Kitchener stitch – you can find the photo tutorial for that on page 112 - then weave in all ends and sew up the small gap at the cuff where you cast on.

Charts - cuff

64 stitches

Left (32 stitches twice)

Right (32 stitches twice)

Key

- ☐ Knit
- ● Purl
- C3B
- C3F

68 stitches

Left (34 stitches twice)

Right (34 stitches twice)

81

72 stitches

Left (36 stitches twice)

Right (36 stitches twice)

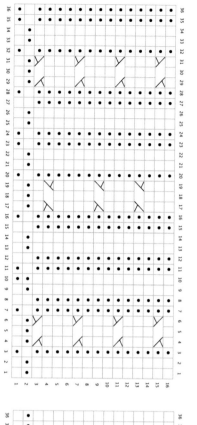

76 stitches

Left (38 stitches twice)

Right (38 stitches twice)

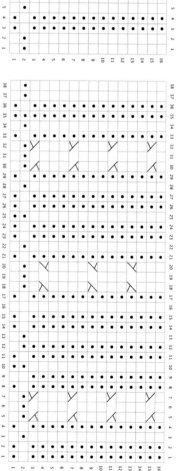

Knit

Purl

C3B

C3F

Charts - leg

64 stitches

Right (32 stitches twice)

Left (32 stitches twice)

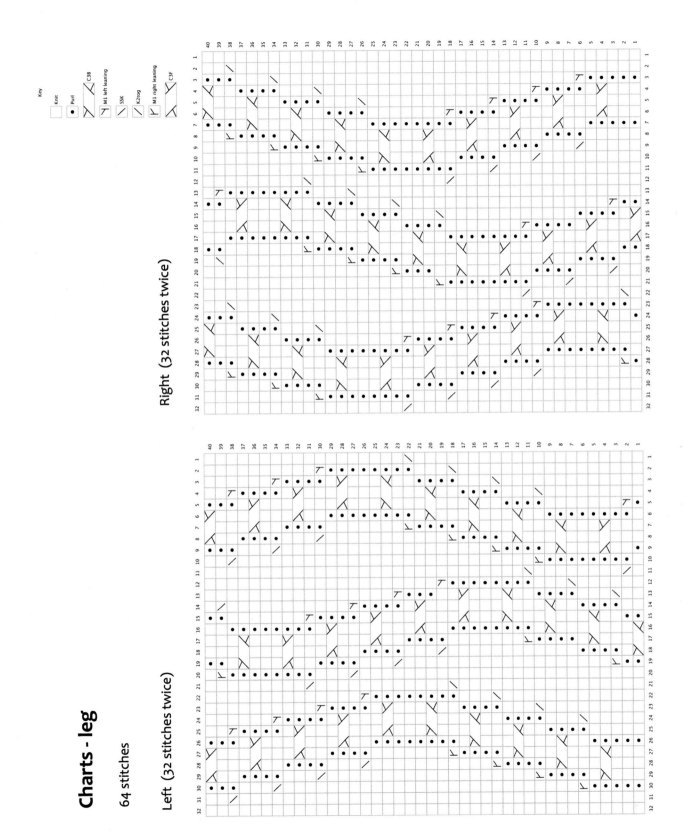

Left (34 stitches twice)

Right (34 stitches twice)

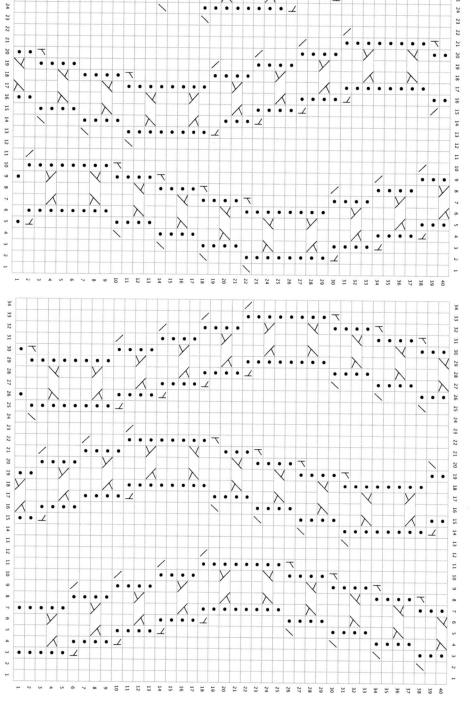

Key

	Knit
●	Purl
╱	M1 left leaning
╲	C3B
⟍	M1 right leaning
⟋	SSk
⟍	K2tog
⟋	M1 right leaning
⟋⟍	C3F

72 stitches

Right (36 stitches twice)

Left (36 stitches twice)

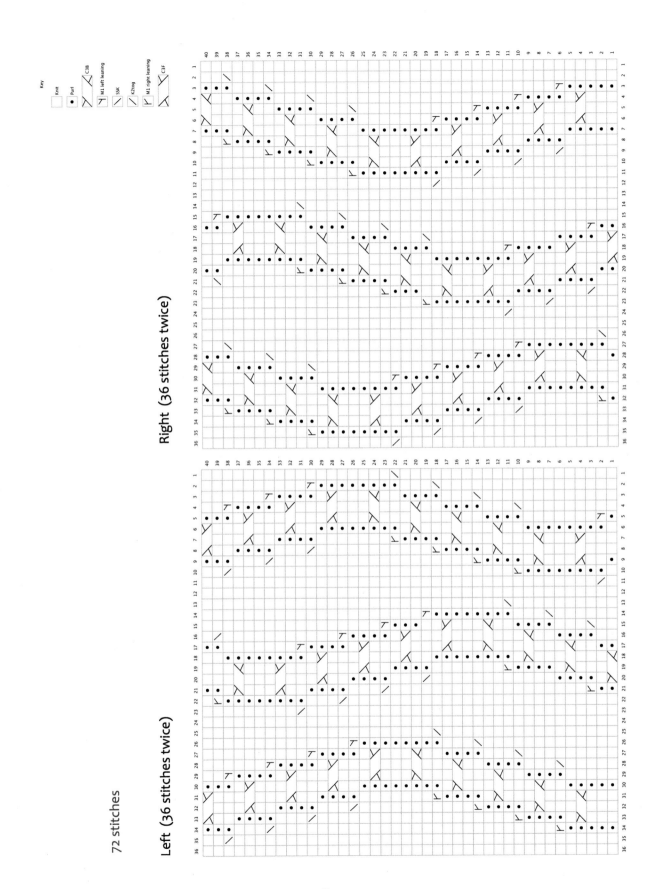

76 stitches

Left (38 stitches twice)

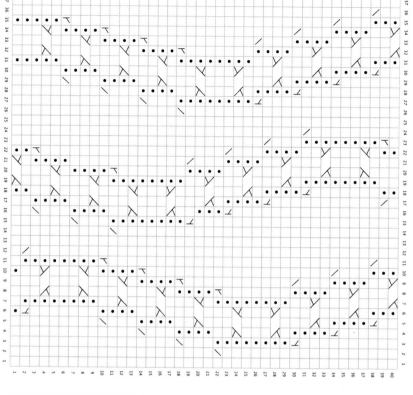

Right (38 stitches twice)

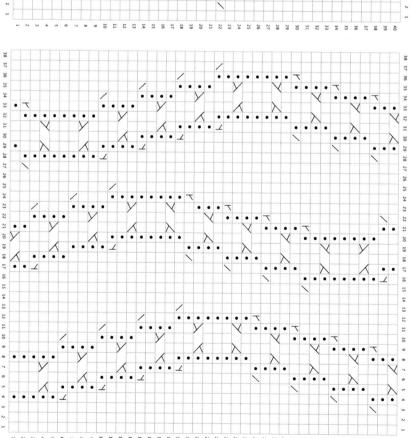

BEATRICE SOCKS

The name "Beatrice" means "bringer of joy and happiness", which is exactly what I hope that these socks will bring to you. These lace socks are perfect for showing off your knitting and sock skills without actually being that difficult to knit – which is always good for our confidence, no matter how experienced a knitter we might be!

These socks are constructed as top down socks with a heel flap and gusset. The heel is knitted in Ribbed Heel Stitch, which creates a durable, cushioned heel and is a more defined rib variation of the traditional Heel Stitch. This pattern is for a medium sized sock, with larger sizes given in parentheses. The length of the sock is easily adjusted for any foot.

The Beatrice Socks pattern works in exactly the same way as the Easy Lace Socks on page 24, so if you were confident in knitting the Easy Lace Socks then you'll have no trouble with this pattern, despite the charts being much bigger and looking more complicated. Have another look at the Easy Lace Socks tutorial if you need a reminder on how to read a chart – don't forget that you're always working from right to left and you're also only working one round at a time so as long as you mark off on your pattern where you're up to (it's fine to make a copy for your own personal use if you'd like to) then you won't get lost.

Size   To fit ball of foot circumference 8 [8.5:9:9.5] inches; 20 [22:23:24] cm

Gauge   30 stitches to 4 inches (10 cm) in stocking stitch (worked in the round) on 2.5 mm needles

Materials

2.5 mm needles – short circular needle, DPNs (double pointed needles) or 80 cm circular for magic loop
2 x 50g ball of Eden Cottage Yarns Milburn 4ply in shade Bramble
1 set DPNs size 3.0 mm (optional)
1 set DPNs size 2.5 mm (not required for magic loop)
Stitch holder (optional)
Stitch markers
Wool needle

Abbreviations

K	Knit
Ktbl	Knit through the back loop of the stitch
K2tog	Knit two stitches together
P	Purl
Slip 1	Slip 1 stitch purlwise
SSK	Slip the first stitch on the left hand needle knitwise onto the right hand needle, slip the second stitch on the left hand needle purlwise onto the right hand needle, slip both stitches back onto the left hand needle and knit together through back loop
St(s)	Stitch(es)
yfwd	Bring the yarn forward from the back of the work between the needles to the front
( )	Repeat instructions within brackets

Pattern Notes

- It is often easier to cast on using DPNs before changing to the short circular needle and joining into the round and so this pattern has been written for this method. If you want to use magic loop you will be able to cast on with the larger circular needle if you prefer to do so, but remember not to pull your cast on stitches too tight. If you use DPNs, you might find it easiest to cast on and work 2 rows before dividing the stitches across the needles.
- Use lifelines in your work as often as you feel you need to – there's no limit to the number of them that you can use in one sock! You can find instructions for creating lifelines on page 33.
- Mark each row on your chart as you work it – it's easier to work out where you're up to if you have to put your knitting down for a while.
- If you have to take your work back, unravel one round at a time and don't forget to amend your chart so that you know where you're up to.

Pattern - make both the same

Cast on 60 [64:68:72] stitches using 3.0 mm double pointed needles.

Row 1:   (Ktbl, P1), repeat to end, turn.
Row 2:   (Ktbl, P1), repeat to end, turn.

Ktbl (knitting through the back loop) is pretty much how it sounds.

Instead of working a "normal" knit stitch where you take the yarn from the front of the needle like this ...

you take your needle round to the back of the stitch and knit into the back leg instead

This twists the stitch and makes the rib more defined.

Change to a 2.5 mm short circular needle, magic loop or divide the stitches across DPNs and join into a circle, place marker. You will sew up the small gap where you knitted the first two rows later.

Continue in Ktbl, P1 rib for 14 more rounds or until desired length of rib.

Leg

Using either the leg chart or the written pattern for your size, work the lace pattern for each round until the leg measures 6 [7] inches; 15 [17] cm or desired length from cast on edge. Move the start of your round if required when you begin the lace pattern so that the central knit stitch of the pattern lines up with a knit stitch on your rib – it looks smarter if you do that! It doesn't matter which round of the pattern you finish on, but you will need to make a note of it so that you can start on the next round when you work the gusset. **Remember to work the pattern section twice for all sizes.**

60 stitches (30 stitches twice)

Round 1 and all odd-numbered rounds: P1, (Ktbl, P2, K4, P1, K4, P2) twice, Ktbl.
Round 2:   P1, (Ktbl, P2, K2, K2tog, yfwd, P1, yfwd, SSK, K2, P2) twice, Ktbl. (30 sts)
Round 4:   P1, (Ktbl, P2, K1, K2tog, yfwd, K1, P1, K1, yfwd, SSK, K1, P2) twice, Ktbl.
Round 6:   P1, (Ktbl, P2, K2tog, yfwd, K2, P1, K2, yfwd, SSK, P2) twice, Ktbl.
Round 8:   P1, (Ktbl, P2, K1, yfwd, K1, K2tog, P1, SSK, K1, yfwd, K1, P2) twice, Ktbl.
Round 10:   Repeat round 8.

64 stitches (32 stitches twice)

Round 1 and all odd-numbered rounds: Ktbl, P1, (Ktbl, P2, K4, P1, K4, P2) twice, Ktbl, P1.
Round 2:   Ktbl, P1, (Ktbl, P2, K2, K2tog, yfwd, P1, yfwd, SSK, K2, P2) twice, Ktbl, P1. (32 sts)
Round 4:   Ktbl, P1, (Ktbl, P2, K1, K2tog, yfwd, K1, P1, K1, yfwd, SSK, K1, P2) twice, Ktbl, P1.
Round 6:   Ktbl, P1, (Ktbl, P2, K2tog, yfwd, K2, P1, K2, yfwd, SSK, P2) twice, Ktbl, P1.
Round 8:   Ktbl, P1, (Ktbl, P2, K1, yfwd, K1, K2tog, P1, SSK, K1, yfwd, K1, P2) twice, Ktbl, P1.
Round 10:   Repeat round 8.

68 stitches (34 stitches twice)

Round 1 and all odd-numbered rounds: P1, Ktbl, P1, (Ktbl, P2, K4, P1, K4, P2) twice, Ktbl, P1, Ktbl.
Round 2:   P1, Ktbl, P1, (Ktbl, P2, K2, K2tog, yfwd, P1, yfwd, SSK, K2, P2) twice, Ktbl, P1, Ktbl. (34 sts)
Round 4:   P1, Ktbl, P1, (Ktbl, P2, K1, K2tog, yfwd, K1, P1, K1, yfwd, SSK, K1, P2) twice, Ktbl, P1, Ktbl.

89

Round 6:   P1, Ktbl, P1, (Ktbl, P2, K2tog, yfwd, K2, P1, K2, yfwd, SSK, P2) twice, Ktbl, P1, Ktbl.
Round 8:   P1, Ktbl, P1, (Ktbl, P2, K1, yfwd, K1, K2tog, P1, SSK, K1, yfwd, K1, P2) twice, Ktbl, P1, Ktbl.
Round 10:   Repeat round 8.

72 stitches (36 stitches twice)

Round 1 and all odd-numbered rounds: (P1, K4, P1, Ktbl, P1, K4) 3 times.
Round 2:   (P1, yfwd, SSK, K2, P1, Ktbl, P1, K2, K2tog, yfwd) 3 times. (36 sts)
Round 4:   (P1, K1, yfwd, SSK, K1, P1, Ktbl, P1, K1, K2tog, yfwd, K1) 3 times.
Round 6:   (P1, K2, yfwd, SSK, P1, Ktbl, P1, K2tog, yfwd, K2) 3 times.
Round 8:   (P1, SSK, K1, yfwd, K1, P1, Ktbl, P1, K1, yfwd, K1, K2tog) 3 times.
Round 10:   Repeat round 8.

Knitting the lace pattern is the same for all the sock sizes. Remember that you're knitting into the back loop (Ktbl) across the pattern to make the knitted stitches more defined. There's a slight difference between round 2 and the other rounds because of the way you create the yarn forward, but other than that, you're not using any stitches that you won't have used before.

Round 2: When you work the yfwd, you bring the yarn to the front of your work between the last stitch on your right hand needle and the first stitch on your left hand needle.

Because the next stitch is a purl stitch, you'll need to take the yarn over the top of the needle and bring it round again to make sure that you've got an extra stitch on your needle – simply purling the stitch on your left hand needle here wouldn't make that extra stitch.

After you've purled the stitch, you can take the yarn over the top of the needle to knit the next stitch and that will give you the extra stitch without you needing to wrap the yarn around twice.

Rounds 4, 6, 8 & 10: When you work the yfwd, you bring the yarn to the front of your work between the last stitch on your right hand needle and the first stitch on your left hand needle.

When you work your next knit stitch, simply take the yarn over the top of the needle to knit the next stitch and that will give you the extra stitch without you needing to wrap the yarn around twice.

Heel Flap

Change to 2.5 mm DPNs if you are using a short circular needle. There is no need to use DPNs if you are using magic loop. You may prefer to place the spare stitches from the top of the foot onto a stitch holder if you are using a short circular or DPNs whilst you work the heel.

Row 1:   K2, (Slip 1, P1) until you have 28 [30:32:34] stitches on your needle, Slip 1, K1, turn. (30:32:34:36 stitches)

Row 2:   Slip 1, (P1, K1) to last 3 stitches, P3, turn.

Row 3:   Slip 1, K1, (Slip 1, P1) to last two stitches, Slip1, K1, turn.

Repeat rows 2 and 3 until heel measures approximately 2 inches (5 cm), finishing on row 3. If you want to make the heel flap longer, continuing knitting rows 2 and 3 until you reach the desired length, but remember that you will need to pick up more stitches to create the gusset.

Turn heel

Row 1:   Slip 1, P16 [P17:P18:P19], P2tog, P1, turn

Row 2:   Slip 1, K5, SSK, K1, turn

Row 3:   Slip 1, P6, P2tog, P1, turn

Row 4:   Slip 1, K7, SSK, K1, turn

Continue in this way, adding one stitch between slip stitch and SSK or P2tog on each row (ie, Row 5: Slip 1, **P8**, P2tog, P1; Row 6: Slip 1, **K9**, SSK, K1, etc) until all of the heel stitches are used.

Knit across heel stitches if required to bring you to the left hand side of the heel flap (with the outside of the flap facing you) ready to pick up 1 stitch for every 2 rows knitted. Remember that if you made the heel flap bigger, you will need to pick up more stitches. Once you have picked up the stitches, place marker. Knit across the top of the foot stitches in pattern (continuing from the row after the one where you finished for your leg), place marker, then pick up 1 stitch for every 2 rows of heel flap knitted up the other side of the heel. Knit across the top of the heel and then shape gusset as follows.

Note: If you are using DPNs and/or have placed your stitches on a stitch holder, you can arrange the needles as follows: Needle 1 for stitches across heel, Needle 2 for picked-up stitches down side of foot, Needle 3 for stitches across top of foot (knit stitches off stitch holder if required), Needle 4 for picked-up stitches on other side of foot. You may find that stitch markers are not required at first.

Shape gusset

To make sure that your pattern stays centred on your sock, you are going to add a stitch to the end of the pattern before you make the SSK decrease. You're not increasing the number of stitches, just moving your stitch marker over to add one more to the total number of stitches. It sounds complicated now but it's very easy!

start of picked up gusset stitches

end of top of the foot pattern stitches

This is how the change to the stitches is going to work:

Once you've started round 1 of the gusset, so you've worked your first K2tog decrease and worked across the top of the foot stitches in pattern, your sock will look like this.

All you're going to do next is take the stitch marker off, slip the next stitch from the left hand needle to the right hand needle and put the stitch marker back on before you work your K1, SSK decrease.

It adds one stitch to the top of the foot stitches without actually increasing the number of stitches on your needle.

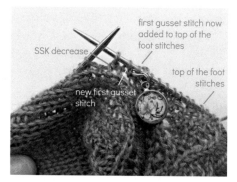

first gusset stitch now added to top of the foot stitches

SSK decrease

top of the foot stitches

new first gusset stitch

Complete round 1 of the gusset shaping in the correct size for your sock and then follow the foot chart or the written pattern for the rest of the foot. Doing this will mean that your SSK decrease is moved one stitch over but it will never be noticed.

60 stitches

Round 1:   K to 3 sts before the marker, K2tog, K1, slip marker, knit in pattern to next marker, remove marker, P1, replace marker, K1, SSK, K to marker.

Round 1:   K to 3 sts before the marker, K2tog, K1, slip marker, knit in pattern to next marker, remove marker, Ktbl, replace marker, K1, SSK, K to marker.

Round 1:   K to 3 sts before the marker, K2tog, K1, slip marker, knit in pattern to next marker, remove marker, P1, replace marker, K1, SSK, K to marker.

Round 1:   K to 3 sts before the marker, K2tog, K1, slip marker, knit in pattern to next marker, remove marker, P1, replace marker, K1, SSK, K to marker.

All sizes:

Round 2:   Slip marker, knit in pattern to next marker, slip marker, knit to 3 sts before marker.
Round 3:   K2tog, K1, slip marker, knit in pattern to next marker, slip marker, K1, SSK, K to marker.

Repeat rounds 2 and 3 to shape the gusset. Continue in this way, decreasing by two stitches at the gusset on every other round until there are 31 [33:35:37] stitches across the top of the foot and 30 [32:34:36] across the sole. (61 [65:69:73] stitches)

Foot pattern – work this pattern once across the top of the foot then knit the rest of the stitches on your needle. Despite the fact that there will be one extra stitch in the sock, I have not renamed the pattern sizes, so continue to follow the same size as before.

60 stitches

Round 1 and all odd-numbered rounds: P1, (Ktbl, P2, K4, P1, K4, P2) twice, Ktbl, P1.
Round 2:   P1, (Ktbl, P2, K2, K2tog, yfwd, P1, yfwd, SSK, K2, P2) twice, Ktbl, P1. (31 sts)
Round 4:   P1, (Ktbl, P2, K1, K2tog, yfwd, K1, P1, K1, yfwd, SSK, K1, P2) twice, Ktbl, P1.
Round 6:   P1, (Ktbl, P2, K2tog, yfwd, K2, P1, K2, yfwd, SSK, P2) twice, Ktbl, P1.
Round 8:   P1, (Ktbl, P2, K1, yfwd, K1, K2tog, P1, SSK, K1, yfwd, K1, P2) twice, Ktbl, P1.
Round 10:   Repeat round 8.

Round 1 and all odd-numbered rounds: Ktbl, P1, (Ktbl, P2, K4, P1, K4, P2) twice, Ktbl, P1, Ktbl.
Round 2:   Ktbl, P1, (Ktbl, P2, K2, K2tog, yfwd, P1, yfwd, SSK, K2, P2) twice, Ktbl, P1, Ktbl. (33 sts)
Round 4:   Ktbl, P1, (Ktbl, P2, K1, K2tog, yfwd, K1, P1, K1, yfwd, SSK, K1, P2) twice, Ktbl, P1, Ktbl.
Round 6:   Ktbl, P1, (Ktbl, P2, K2tog, yfwd, K2, P1, K2, yfwd, SSK, P2) twice, Ktbl, P1, Ktbl.
Round 8:   Ktbl, P1, (Ktbl, P2, K1, yfwd, K1, K2tog, P1, SSK, K1, yfwd, K1, P2) twice, Ktbl, P1, Ktbl.
Round 10:   Repeat round 8.

68 stitches

Round 1 and all odd-numbered rounds: P1, Ktbl, P1, (Ktbl, P2, K4, P1, K4, P2) twice, (Ktbl, P1) twice.
Round 2:   P1, Ktbl, P1, (Ktbl, P2, K2, K2tog, yfwd, P1, yfwd, SSK, K2, P2) twice, (Ktbl, P1) twice. (35 sts)
Round 4:   P1, Ktbl, P1, (Ktbl, P2, K1, K2tog, yfwd, K1, P1, K1, yfwd, SSK, K1, P2) twice, (Ktbl, P1) twice.
Round 6:   P1, Ktbl, P1, (Ktbl, P2, K2tog, yfwd, K2, P1, K2, yfwd, SSK, P2) twice, (Ktbl, P1) twice.
Round 8:   P1, Ktbl, P1, (Ktbl, P2, K1, yfwd, K1, K2tog, P1, SSK, K1, yfwd, K1, P2) twice, (Ktbl, P1) twice.
Round 10:   Repeat round 8.

72 stitches

Round 1 and all odd-numbered rounds: (P1, K4, P1, Ktbl, P1, K4) 3 times, P1.
Round 2:   (P1, yfwd, SSK, K2, P1, Ktbl, P1, K2, K2tog, yfwd) 3 times, P1. (37 sts)
Round 4:   (P1, K1, yfwd, SSK, K1, P1, Ktbl, P1, K1, K2tog, yfwd, K1) 3 times, P1.
Round 6:   (P1, K2, yfwd, SSK, P1, Ktbl, P1, K2tog, yfwd, K2) 3 times, P1.
Round 8:   (P1, SSK, K1, yfwd, K1, P1, Ktbl, P1, K1, yfwd, K1, K2tog) 3 times, P1.
Round 10:   Repeat round 8.

Once you have reached the required number of stitches, continue to knit each round (incorporating the pattern across the top of the foot) without decreasing until you reach approximately 2 inches (5 cm) before the desired length ready to start the toes. Don't be afraid to try your sock on before decreasing for the toes!

Toes

Note: At some point whilst decreasing for the toes, if you are using a short circular needle you may need to change back to DPNs or use the magic loop method as the number of stitches becomes too small for the circular. It's up to you when you choose to do that, and how you distribute the stitches across the needles; just keep following the pattern as set below.

I chose to work the toes in twisted rib, lining up the knit stitches with the pattern but you can use plain knit if you prefer. If you use the twisted rib, work the stitches so that they line up with your own pattern – it will be different for each sock depending on where you finished the lace pattern. **Important!** There will be one extra stitch on the top of the foot where you added it in at the gusset to keep the pattern straight. You're going to keep that extra stitch in for now so that your toe pattern stays centred and then decrease it at the very end – don't worry, it won't be seen! It will mean that you're working with an odd number of stitches across the top of the foot.

Create the toes as follows, starting the decreases on the top of the foot:

Round 1:   K1, SSK, K25 [27:29:31] sts in twisted rib matching knit stitches with foot pattern, K2tog, K1, place marker, K1, SSK, K24 [26:28:30] sts, K2tog, K1. (57:61:65:69) sts – remember there is one extra stitch across the top of the foot!)
Round 2:   K2, work in twisted rib until 2 sts before end of first toe section, K2, K to end of round, slipping markers as you come to them.
Round 3:   K1, SSK, K to 3 sts before marker in twisted rib, K2tog, K1, slip marker, K1, SSK, K to 3 sts before marker, K2tog, K1. (53 [57:61:65] sts)

94

Repeat rounds 2 and 3 until you have 29 stitches left ending on round 3, then decrease 1 stitch at start of next round and work as for round 2 (28 stitches). Divide these between two needles so that front and back of socks match.

Graft the toes using Kitchener stitch – you can find the photo tutorial for that on page 112 - then weave in all ends and sew up the small gap at the cuff where you cast on.

Charts - leg

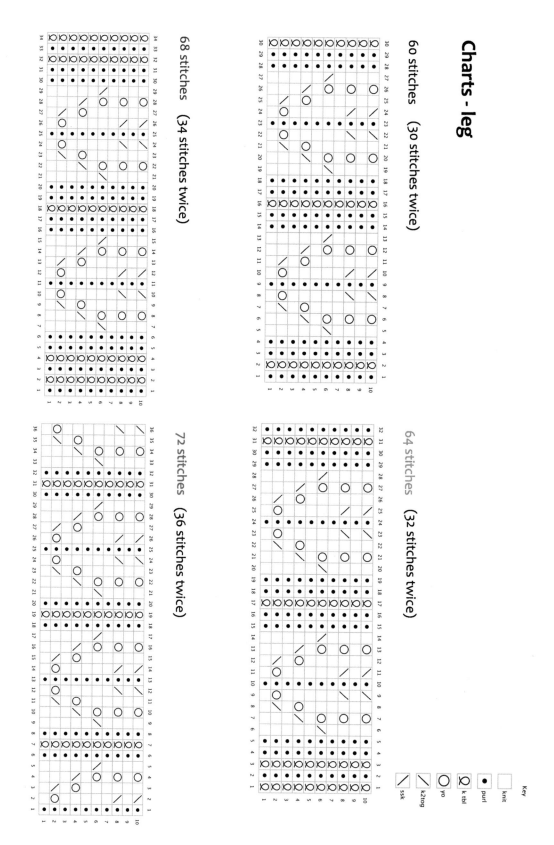

60 stitches (30 stitches twice)

64 stitches (32 stitches twice)

68 stitches (34 stitches twice)

72 stitches (36 stitches twice)

Key

☐	knit
●	purl
Ｑ	k tbl
○	yo
╱	k2tog
╲	ssk

Charts - foot

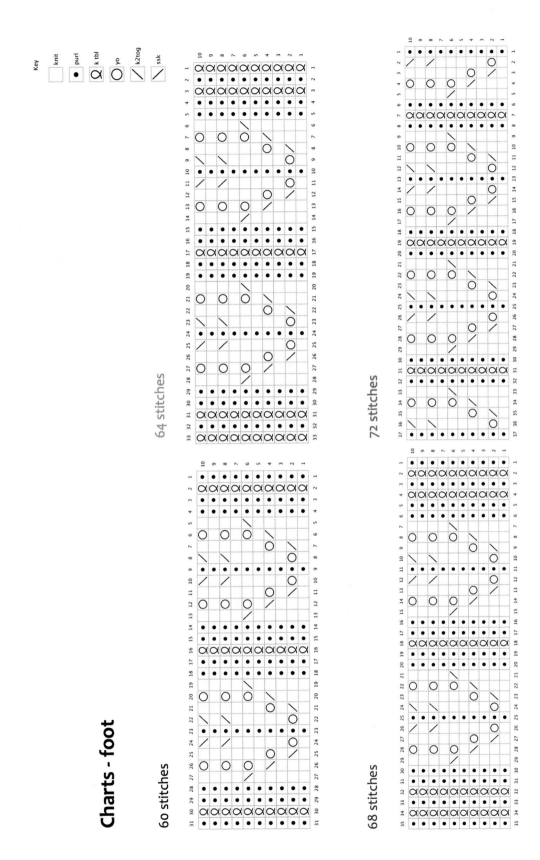

60 stitches

64 stitches

68 stitches

72 stitches

FLOW THROUGH SOCKS

Knitters know all about leftover yarns and these socks work beautifully with them! I loved the idea of combining a striped yarn with solid colours. The changes in the striped yarn "flow through" between the solid colours, giving the effect of that section moving more quickly down the sock. Have fun with your own combinations!

These socks are constructed as top down socks with a heel flap and gusset. The heel is knitted in ribbed heel stitch, which creates a durable, cushioned heel. These socks are knitted using the intarsia method and because the socks are knitted in the round, a wrap and turn is used which means that every other round will be a purl round.

Size   To fit ball of foot circumference 8 [8.5:9:9.5] inches; 20 [22:23:24] cm

Gauge   30 stitches to 4 inches (10cm) in stocking stitch (worked in the round) on 2.5 mm needles

Materials

2.5 mm needles – short circular needle, DPNs (Double Pointed Needles) or an 80 cm circular for magic loop
100g of 4ply sock yarn in different colours (leftovers are perfect!) – *I used West Yorkshire Spinners Signature 4ply yarn in Milk Bottle (Main colour, MC), Violet (Contrast colour 1, CC1), Pink Flamingo (Contrast colour 2, CC2), and Blackcurrant Bomb (Contrast colour 3, CC3)*
1 set DPNs size 3.0 mm (optional)
1 set DPNs size 2.5 mm (not required for magic loop)
Stitch holder (optional)
Stitch markers
Wool needle

Abbreviations

K	Knit
K2tog	Knit two stitches together
Slip 1	Slip 1 stitch purlwise
SSK	Slip the first stitch on the left hand needle knitwise onto the right hand needle, slip the second stitch on the left hand needle purlwise onto the right hand needle, slip both stitches back onto the left hand needle and knit together through back loop
P	Purl

P2togtbl	Purl the next two stitches together by putting your right hand needle through the stitches from left to right at the back of the left hand needle. As an alternative, you can use knitting expert Barbara Walker's method of purling the next stitch on the left hand needle, slipping the purled stitch back onto the left hand needle and slipping the second stitch on the left hand needle over the purled stitch can be used instead.
St(s)	Stitch(es)
( )	Repeat the instructions inside the brackets

Pattern Notes

- It is often easier to cast on using DPNs before changing to the short circular needle and joining into the round and so this pattern has been written for this method. If you want to use magic loop you will be able to cast on with the larger circular needle if you prefer to do so, but remember not to pull your cast on stitches too tight. If you use DPNs, you might find it easiest to cast on and work 2 rows before dividing the stitches across the needles.
- Use lifelines in your work as often as you feel you need to – there's no limit to the number of them that you can use in one sock! You can find instructions for creating lifelines on page 33.
- Mark each row on your chart as you work it – it's easier to work out where you're up to if you have to put your knitting down for a while.
- If you have to take your work back, unravel one round at a time and don't forget to amend your chart so that you know where you're up to.

Pattern

Using MC, cast on 60 [64:68:72] stitches using 3.0 mm double pointed needles.

Row 1:   (K2, P2), repeat to end, turn.
Row 2:   (K2, P2), repeat to end, turn.

Change to 2.5 mm needles. At this point, change to a short circular needle, magic loop or divide the stitches across DPNs and join into a circle; place marker.

Continue in K2, P2 rib for 14 more rounds or until desired length of rib.

Leg

This sock uses the intarsia method to join the colours at each section, and a wrap and turn is used at the end of the round. You should read this section first before knitting. The photo and video tutorial on working the intarsia sections is in the Patchwork Socks pattern on page 37.

Work both legs the same. I have chosen to reverse the colours for the second sock but it's your choice whether to do that or not. Because you are not knitting in the round as the same way as usual, you need to **read the colour chart from right to left on knit rounds and left to right on purl rounds.**

I have written these instructions to include the use of a stitch marker on the leg and foot sections, but you may find that it becomes easier not to use one as you will use the wrapped stitches as your marker. If that's the case for you, don't worry about taking the stitch marker off as you will always know where the start and end of your round is by the wrapped stitches.

Using the chart for your size and reading the chart from right to left, join the yarn for the new colours as you come to them (I always weave the ends in as I go). I found it easiest to work with long lengths of yarn rather than balls as the yarns will tangle. You will need a new length of the main colour for each section of that colour; you can carry the yarn across if you'd prefer but I found that the finished result wasn't as good as using a separate piece of yarn for each colour. Remember to twist the yarns as you join them so that you don't get a hole where the colours meet.

Work until you reach the end of the round then slip the stitch marker from the left needle to the right, slip the first stitch after the marker to the right hand needle, wrap the yarn around the stitch (not the needle) bringing it from the back of the sock to the front, slip the stitch back from the right hand needle to the left, slip the stitch marker back to the left hand needle and turn your sock.

Note: don't pull the yarn too tightly when you wrap the stitch – if you leave it quite loose it's easier to adjust the stitches later so that the join is not as noticeable. You are going to purl the next round so continue the wrap to bring the yarn to the front of your work, then follow the instructions for all purl rounds.

Follow these instructions for all purl rounds

Reading the chart from left to right, purl across all stitches until you reach the end of the round, twisting the yarns as you change colours so that you don't get a hole. When you reach the wrapped stitch at the end of the round, pick up the wrapped yarn and purl it together with the stitch it was wrapped around. Slip the marker, slip the next stitch from the left hand needle to the right hand needle, wrap the yarn around the stitch (not the needle) bringing it from the front of the sock to the back, slip the stitch back from the right hand needle to the left, slip the stitch marker back to the left hand needle and turn your sock. **Note:** don't pull the yarn too tightly when you wrap the stitch – if you leave it quite loose it's easier to adjust the stitches later so that the join is not as noticeable. You are going to knit the next round so continue the wrap to bring the yarn to the back of your work, then follow the instructions for all knit rounds.

Follow these instructions for all knit rounds

Reading the chart from right to left, knit across all stitches until you reach the end of the round, twisting the yarns as you change colours so that you don't get a hole. When you reach the wrapped stitch at the end of the round, pick up the wrapped yarn and knit it together with the stitch it was wrapped around. Slip the stitch marker from the left needle to the right, slip the first stitch after the marker to the right hand needle, wrap the yarn around the stitch (not the needle) bringing it from the back of the sock to the front, slip the stitch back from the right hand needle to the left, slip the stitch marker back to the left hand needle and turn your sock. **Note:** don't pull the yarn too tightly when you wrap the stitch – if you leave it quite loose it's easier to adjust the stitches later so that the join is not as noticeable. You are going to purl the next round so continue the wrap to bring the yarn to the front of your work, then follow the instructions for all purl rounds.

Note: If you prefer not to knit or purl the wraps that's fine – you can leave them as wraps and just knit the stitches instead - but you will see them on the outside of your sock. That's a design feature of your choice! ☺

When you get to the sections where the main colour yarn is carried across the coloured block, I found it easiest so use the first main colour yarn to knit all of the main colour stitches in that section – that way you don't get any break in the colour where you've changed the yarn.

As you work back along the section, simply carry the "spare" main colour yarn up your knitting and anchor it with your working yarn to stop you having a long float on that section. You will go back to using the two lengths of main colour yarn on the next round.

Continue to knit or purl each round until you reach the desired length before start of heel (for me, this is usually around 72 rounds in total including the rib), remembering which row you finished at on the chart as you will need this later.

Heel Flap – make both the same

Change to 2.5 mm DPNs if you are using a short circular needle. To create the heel flap on the other side of the sock so that the joins of each sock will be on different sides (ie, both on the inside or both on the outside), work 30 [32:34:36] stitches in pattern before you start the flap on the second sock.

Using MC, work two rows of stocking stitch then work heel flap as follows:

Row 1:   K2, (Slip 1, K1) until you have 30 [32:34:36] stitches on your needle, turn.
Row 2:   Slip 1, P to end, turn.
Row 3:   (Slip 1, K1) to end, turn.

Repeat rows 2 and 3 until heel flap measures approximately 2 inches (5 cm), finishing on row 3 (for me this is approx 35 rows). If you want to make the heel flap longer, continue knitting rows 2 and 3 until you reach the desired length, but remember that you will need to pick up more stitches to create the gusset.

Turn heel

Using MC, turn heel as follows:

Row 1:   Slip 1, P16 [P17:P18:P19], P2tog, P1, turn.
Row 2:   Slip 1, K5, SSK, K1, turn.
Row 3:   Slip 1, P6, P2tog, P1, turn.
Row 4:   Slip 1, K7, SSK, K1, turn.

Continue in this way, adding one stitch between slip stitch and SSK or P2tog on each row (ie, Row 5: Slip 1, **P8**, P2tog, P1; Row 6: Slip 1, **K9**, SSK, K1, etc) until all of the heel stitches are used.

Gusset

Using MC, you are going to pick up and knit 1 stitch for every 2 rows knitted down the **left hand side** of your heel flap. Remember that if you made the heel flap bigger, you will need to pick up more stitches. Once you have picked up the stitches, place marker.

Knit across the top of the foot stitches in pattern – use a new length of main colour yarn if required at the start rather than using the working yarn so that you don't end up with your working yarn on the wrong side of the join. If you find that the contrast yarn is at the wrong side of each block of colour, simply bring the yarn across the back of the sock so that you can use it to knit with, and then anchor the yarn under the working yarn as you knit so that the float won't catch on your toes as you put your sock on.

When you have worked the top of the foot stitches, place marker then pick up and knit 1 stitch for every 2 rows of heel flap knitted up the other side of the heel. You can use the existing main colour yarn from the end of the pattern block for these stitches. Knit across the top of the heel stitches and then shape gusset as below.

Note: If you are using DPNs and/or have placed your stitches on a stitch holder, you can arrange the needles as follows: Needle 1 for stitches across heel, Needle 2 for picked-up stitches down side of foot, Needle 3 for stitches across top of foot (knit stitches off stitch holder if required), Needle 4 for picked-up stitches on other side of foot. You may find that stitch markers are not required at first.

Shape gusset

Round 1:   K to 3 sts before the end of the first set of picked up stitches, K2tog, slip the next stitch from the left hand needle to the right, wrap yarn around next stitch, turn and slip marker. Drop the yarn that you are using if it is a length of yarn rather than the main ball and instead use the main colour yarn from the ball which you used to pick up the stitches so that you won't have to join a new length of yarn across the sole of your foot. Purl along the stitches until 3 sts before next marker, P2togtbl, P1, slip marker, purl across top of foot stitches in pattern to wrapped stitch, pick up the wrap and purl the stitch and the wrap together, slip marker, wrap the yarn around stitch you have just purled, slip it back onto the left hand needle, turn and slip marker.

Round 2:   Knit in pattern to next marker, slip marker, knit to 3 sts before marker.

Round 3:   K2tog, pick up the wrap and knit the stitch and the wrap together, slip marker, slip the next stitch from the left hand needle to the right, wrap yarn around the stitch, slip the stitch from the right needle to the left, turn and slip stitch marker. Purl back along the stitches until 3 stitches before next marker, P2togtbl, P1, slip marker, purl across top of foot stitches in pattern to wrapped stitch, pick up the wrap and purl the stitch and the wrap together, slip marker, wrap the yarn around stitch you have just purled, slip it back onto the left hand needle, turn and slip marker.

Repeat rounds 2 and 3 to shape the gusset. Continue in this way, decreasing by two stitches at the gusset on every other row until there are 60 [64:68:72] stitches on the needle.

Once you have reached the required number of stitches, continue to knit and purl each round in pattern until you reach approximately 2 inches (5 cm) before the desired length ready to start the toes. For my size 5 feet, this is about 45 rounds. Don't be afraid to try your sock on before decreasing for the toes!

Toes

At some point whilst decreasing for the toes, if you are using a short circular you may need to change to DPNs or use magic loop as the number of stitches becomes too small for the circular. It's up to you when you choose to do that, and how you distribute the stitches across the needles; just keep following the pattern as set below. If you have cast on more or less than 60 stitches you will need to adjust the number of stitches between the decreases to accommodate this.

I chose to knit my toes in one colour, but you can continue the blocks of colour if you would prefer. To knit plain toes, knit one round in the colour you want your toes to be, cutting the yarns and weaving the ends in as you go. There is no need to continue the wrap and turn method for the toes; knit each round to create the toes as follows:

Round 1:   K1, SSK, K24 [26:28:30] sts, K2tog, K1, place marker, K1, SSK, K24 [26:28:30] sts, K2tog, K1.
            (56 [60:64:68] sts)
Round 2:   Knit one round, slipping markers as you come to them.
Round 3:   K1, SSK, K to 3 sts before marker, K2tog, K1, slip marker, K1, SSK, K to 3 sts before marker, K2tog, K1.
            (52 [56:60:64] sts)

Repeat rounds 2 and 3 until you have 28 stitches left and divide these between two needles so that front and back of socks match.

Graft the toes using Kitchener stitch – you can find the photo tutorial for that on page 112 - then weave in all ends and sew up the small gap at the cuff where you cast on. If your join looks a bit loose, you can also use the method from the Patchwork Socks tutorial on page 37 to wiggle the stitches into a better position.

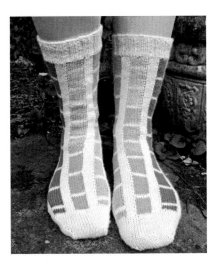

Charts

60 stitches (30 stitches twice)

Reverse contrast colours 1 and 3 for second sock

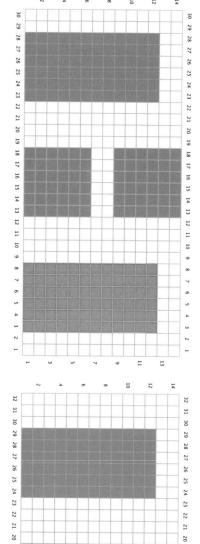

64 stitches (32 stitches twice)

Reverse contrast colours 1 and 3 for second sock

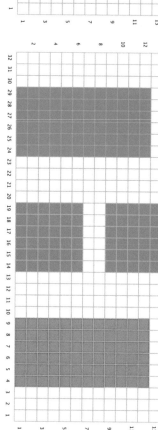

Key

Main colour
Contrast colour 1
Contrast colour 2
Contrast colour 3

68 stitches (34 stitches twice)

Reverse contrast colours 1 and 3 for second sock

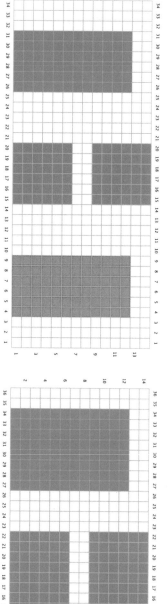

72 stitches (36 stitches twice)

Reverse contrast colours 1 and 3 for second sock

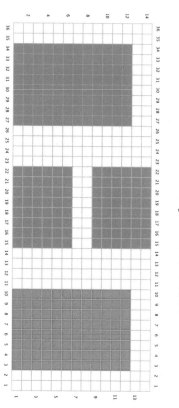

RAINBOW ZIG ZAG SOCKS

Don't you just love a rainbow? There's something about those colours together that never fail to make me smile, and the contrast of the colours against the dark background makes my heart very happy. The colours run down the heel and onto the bottom of the sock so that your whole foot is wrapped in colour!

These socks are constructed as top down socks with a heel flap and gusset. The heel is created in alternating stripes of colour which gives a cushioned heel without needing to use the traditional heel stitch, although it is possible to substitute this if preferred. This pattern is for a medium sized sock, with larger sizes suitable for men and women given in parentheses. The length of the sock is easily adjusted for any foot.

Size   To fit ball of foot circumference 8 [8.5:9:9.5] inches; 20 [22:23:24] cm

Gauge   30 stitches to 4 inches (10 cm) in stocking stitch (worked in the round) on 2.5 mm needles

Materials

2.5 mm needles – short circular needle, DPNs (double pointed needles) or 80 cm circular for magic loop
1 x 100g ball of West Yorkshire Spinners Signature 4ply Liquorice (Main colour, MC)
1 x 100g ball of West Yorkshire Spinners Signature 4ply Rum Paradise (Contrast colour, CC)
1 set DPNs size 3.0 mm (optional)
1 set DPNs size 2.5 mm (not required for magic loop)
Stitch holder (optional)
Stitch markers
Wool needle

Abbreviations

K	Knit
K2tog	Knit two stitches together
P	Purl
Slip 1	Slip 1 stitch purlwise
SSK	Slip the first stitch on the left hand needle knitwise onto the right hand needle, slip the second stitch on the left hand needle purlwise onto the right hand needle, slip both stitches back onto the left hand needle and knit together through back loop
St(s)	Stitch(es)
( )	Repeat instructions inside brackets

Pattern Notes

- It is often easier to cast on using DPNs before changing to the short circular needle and joining into the round and so this pattern has been written for this method. If you want to use magic loop you will be able to cast on with the larger circular needle if you prefer to do so, but remember not to pull your cast on stitches too tight. If you use DPNs, you might find it easiest to cast on and work 2 rows before dividing the stitches across the needles.
- Use lifelines in your work as often as you feel you need to – there's no limit to the number of them that you can use in one sock! You can find instructions for creating lifelines on page 33.
- Mark each row on your chart as you work it – it's easier to work out where you're up to if you have to put your knitting down for a while.
- If you have to take your work back, unravel one round at a time and don't forget to amend your chart so that you know where you're up to.

Before you start: this pattern uses stranded colourwork to create the rainbow effect and whilst in theory this should not make your sock any smaller, it is very easy to pull the floats a little tight and for this reason you might want to consider casting on the next size up. Alternatively, if you are a confident colourwork knitter but want to be sure that the gusset doesn't become too tight, simply make your heel flap a little longer than usual (thereby picking up more stitches and decreasing for more rounds) and this should solve the problem. I don't recommend carrying your floats for any more than 4 stitches so that you won't have any issues with getting your toes stuck in them when you put your socks on. If you need to carry the float for more than 4 stitches, anchor it by twisting the working yarn and contrast yarn together so that the float is not so long.

Pattern

Using West Yorkshire Spinners Signature 4ply in Liquorice (MC), cast on 60 [64:68:72] stitches using 3.0 mm double pointed needles.

Row 1:   (K2, P2), repeat to end, turn.
Row 2:   (K2, P2), repeat to end, turn.

Change to a 2.5 mm short circular needle, magic loop or divide the stitches across DPNs and join into a circle, place marker. You will sew up the small gap where you knitted the first two rows later.

Continue in K2, P2 rib for 14 more rounds or until desired length of rib.

Left leg

Using the left leg chart in the correct size, join Rum Paradise (CC) and continue to knit each round until leg measures 6 [7] inches; 15 [17] cm or desired length from cast on edge, remembering which round of the zig zag pattern you finished on for the heel as you will need this later. If you need help with knitting with two colours, you'll find the photo tutorial and videos from the Easy Colourwork Socks on page 51 useful.

Right leg - Knit the leg section as above, using the chart for the right leg.

<u>Heel Flap</u> – make both the same

Change to 2.5 mm DPNs if you are using a short circular needle. There is no need to use DPNs if you are using magic loop. You may prefer to place the spare stitches from the top of the foot onto a stitch holder if you are using a short circular or DPNs whilst you work the heel.

Row 1:   (K1 in MC, K1 in CC) until you have 30 [32:34:36] stitches on your needle, turn.
Row 2:   Slip 1, P to end in alternate colours to match those already knitted, turn.
Row 3:   Slip 1, K to end in alternate colours to match those already knitted, turn.

Repeat rows 2 and 3 until heel measures approximately 2 inches (5 cm), finishing on row 3. If you want to make the heel flap longer, continuing knitting rows 2 and 3 until you reach the desired length, but remember that you will need to pick up more stitches to create the gusset.

Don't worry that your heel flap won't be as sturdy as a heel stitch heel flap as you're using two yarns which will create a similar effect. This is how your heel flap will look on the outside …

and on the inside.

It is not necessary to cut yarn CC unless you want to match the yarn at a different point when you re-start the pattern on the top of the foot.

<u>Turn heel</u>

Using MC, work the heel turn as follows:

Row 1:   Slip 1, P16 [P17:P18:P19], P2tog, P1, turn.
Row 2:   Slip 1, K5, SSK, K1, turn.
Row 3:   Slip 1, P6, P2tog, P1, turn.
Row 4:   Slip 1, K7, SSK, K1, turn.

Continue in this way, adding one stitch between slip stitch and SSK or P2tog on each row (ie, Row 5: Slip 1, **P8**, P2tog, P1; Row 6: Slip 1, **K9**, SSK, K1 etc) until all of the heel stitches are used.

Knit across the heel stitches if required to bring you to the left hand side of the heel flap (with the outside of the flap facing you) ready to pick up and knit the gusset stitches. You'll need both of your colours but you're only going to knit with MC for now.

You'll notice that you have one big stitch in colour to pick up and knit down the heel flap, but not enough of them to create a full-sized gusset – working the heel flap as we have done means that the heel flap isn't quite the same as one worked in heel stitch. Pick up and knit a new stitch into the front and back legs of each coloured stitch (so that's two stitches to each one), carrying the contrast yarn down the side of the heel flap as you pick up the stitches, ready to start the pattern across the top of the foot.

You will need to anchor the yarn as you may have done whilst working the leg so that the floats don't catch on your toes as you put your sock on. Remember that if you made the heel flap bigger, you will need to pick up more stitches. Once you have picked up the stitches, place marker. Knit across the top of the foot stitches in pattern using yarn CC where required, place marker, then pick up and knit 2 stitches into every large slipped stitch of heel flap up the other side of the heel in MC, carrying yarn CC as you go, anchoring the yarn as necessary.

Knit across the top of the heel in alternate colours to match the heel flap. It'll be easy for you to follow the sequence to work the alternating colours down the side of the heel flap to match when you start the gusset shaping.

match the colour sequence up with the heel flap

Note: If you are using DPNs and/or have placed your stitches on a stitch holder, you can arrange the needles as follows: Needle 1 for stitches across heel, Needle 2 for picked-up stitches down side of foot, Needle 3 for stitches across top of foot (knit stitches off stitch holder if required), Needle 4 for picked-up stitches on other side of foot. You may find that stitch markers are not required at first.

Shape gusset

Round 1:   K in alternate colours following sequence from heel to 3 sts before the marker, then using MC, K2tog, K1, slip marker, knit in zig zag pattern to next marker, slip marker, using MC, K1, SSK, K to 2 sts from marker in alternate colours to match sequence on heel, K2 MC.

Round 2:   Slip marker, knit in zig zag pattern to next marker, slip marker, K2 MC, knit in alternating colour sequence to 3 sts before marker.

Round 3:   Using MC, K2tog, K1, slip marker, knit in zig zag pattern to next marker, slip marker, using MC, K1, SSK, K in alternating colour sequence to marker.

Repeat rounds 2 and 3 to shape the gusset. Continue in this way, decreasing by two stitches at the gusset on every other round until there are 60 [64:68:72] stitches on the needle.

Once you have reached the required number of stitches, continue to knit each round until you reach approximately 2 inches (5 cm) before the desired length ready to start the toes. Don't be afraid to try your sock on before decreasing for the toes!

Toes

Note: At some point whilst decreasing for the toes, if you are using a short circular needle you may need to change back to DPNs or use the magic loop method as the number of stitches becomes too small for the circular. It's up to you when you choose to do that, and how you distribute the stitches across the needles; just keep following the pattern as set below.

If you prefer to continue the pattern down across the toes, it is possible to do that but you will need to take the decreases into account. The pattern has been written for one colour.

Using yarn MC, create the toes as follows:

Round 1: K1, SSK, K24 [26:28:30] sts, K2tog, K1, place marker, K1, SSK, K24 [26:28:30] sts, K2tog, K1. (56 [60:64:68] sts)

Round 2: Knit one round, slipping markers as you come to them

Round 3: K1, SSK, K to 3 sts before marker, K2tog, K1, slip marker, K1, SSK, K to 3 sts before marker, K2tog, K1. (52 [56:60:64] sts)

Repeat rounds 2 and 3 until you have 28 stitches left and divide these between two needles so that front and back of socks match.

Graft the toes using Kitchener stitch – you can find the photo tutorial for that on page 112 - then weave in all ends and sew up the small gap at the cuff where you cast on.

Charts

60 stitches

Left (30 stitches twice)

Right (30 stitches twice)

64 stitches

Left (32 stitches twice)

Right (32 stitches twice)

Key

Main colour

Contrast colour

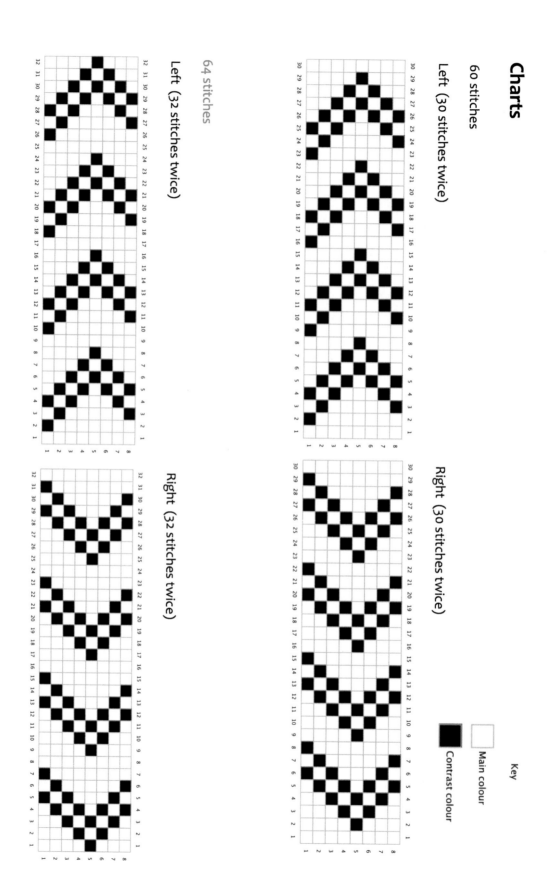

110

Key

Main colour

Contrast colour

68 stitches

Left (34 stitches twice)

Right (34 stitches twice)

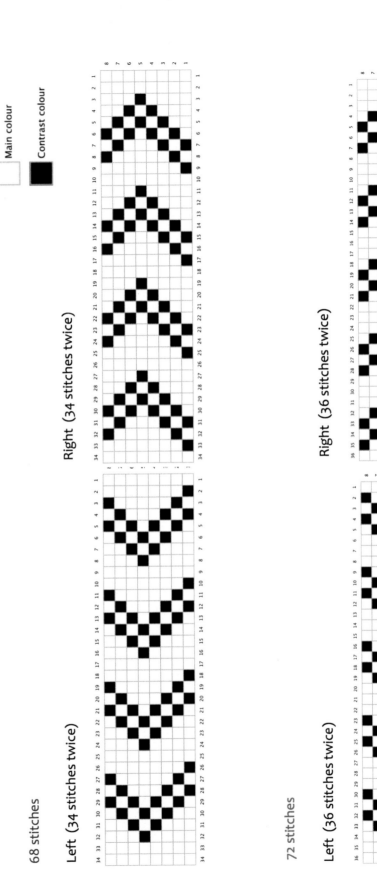

72 stitches

Left (36 stitches twice)

Right (36 stitches twice)

KITCHENER STITCH

When you have finished your sock, the perfect way to join the toes without a seam is to use Kitchener stitch. It's a way of sewing the stitches together so that they look like another stitch has been knitted between them and won't give you any lumpy, bumpy edges that will feel uncomfortable in your shoes.

Kitchener stitch is one part of the sock-creation that some people aren't so keen on, but it's not too bad if you take it slowly and make sure that you're not going to be disturbed. If you're worried that you won't get it right first time, use a lifeline – you can find the instructions for creating those in the Easy Lace Socks tutorial on page 24.

Traditionally, there are two set-up stitches to Kitchener stitch but some people find that using them gives them "ears" on each end of their sock toes which stick out unattractively, so I'm going to show you how to do the set-up stitches but you can miss them out if you'd rather.

OK, here we go! I'm giving you right-handed instructions here.

Here's your sock all ready to start grafting the toes. You've got your stitches evenly distributed across two needles to create the top and bottom of your sock.

Start by cutting a long length from the working yarn – about 10-12 inches (25.5-30 cm) and thread it onto a wool needle.

Set-up stitches – if you're worried about "ears", jump straight to number 3!

1 Hold the two DPNs with your left hand. Insert the wool needle *purl-wise* into the first stitch on the front DPN and pull the yarn through. Don't take the stitch off the DPN.

2 Insert the wool needle *knit-wise* into the first stitch on the back DPN. Don't take the stitch off the DPN.

3 Insert the wool needle *knit-wise* into the first stitch on the front DPN and slip it off.

4 Insert the wool needle *purl-wise* into the second stitch on the front DPN and don't slip it off.

5 Insert the wool needle *purl-wise* into the first stitch on the back DPN and slip it off.

6 Insert the wool needle *knit-wise* into the second stitch on the back DPN and don't slip it off.

Repeat steps 3 to 6 until you get to the last two stitches on the DPNs. You will already have taken the yarn through the front stitch so after you have taken the yarn through the back stitch, you can slip both stitches off the DPN. The single yarn thread through the first stitch will be strong enough to hold it and it will sit flatter when you weave the end back into your sock.

Weave the end securely into the sock and cut the yarn.

THE END?

No, not at all!

This is just the beginning! Now that you've had the chance to practice some more techniques, I hope that you'll feel able to apply your new skills to other patterns and really see how far your sock knitting will take you! Don't forget that you can apply your new chart-reading skills to other project patterns too so there's no end to what you'll find yourself making now! Once you can knit socks, you can knit anything! ☺

I always love to know how people are getting on with their socks, so why not keep in touch?

You can find my blog at **www.winwickmum.co.uk**.

You can find me on Facebook at **Winwick Mum**: the Sockalong group for help with knitting the basic Sockalong sock is at **Winwick Mum Sockalong** and the online knit n natter group for everything else (including the socks from this new book) at **Winwick Mum Knit n Natter**.

You can find me on Ravelry as **Winwick Mum**.

Finally, I'm on Instagram as **Winwick Mum** – the hashtag to show off your new socks is #winwickmumsocks and you'll also find individual hashtags for each of the sock names if you search for them.

Phew! I'm all over the place! It'll be great to see you there too! ☺

INDEX

Made in the USA
San Bernardino, CA
29 September 2018